Introduction

This book of short stories and confessions are mostly written from first-hand experience, though one or two have been related to, or had details confirmed to me by a family member. I hope you'll find them amusing and entertaining though a few are sad memories that I felt inclined to include so they aren't lost for ever. Some stories are confessional in nature and at least one has never been told before. This isn't because there is anything particularly scandalous about them, simply that an opportunity never arose to tell them. Possibly a large number of the actions that took place that created the story should not be attempted without the presence of a 'grown-up', and probably not at all. For the most part, the names haven't been changed to protect the guilty and are in fact the actions of people living or dead, often myself. It's no accident most of my 'motoring stories' aren't included here, but one day some of them may be presented as 'fiction' in a fiction book.

Contents

Trouble with measles

As a kid I grow up with a big sister, at least before my younger brother was born. Since she was a full two years older than me, I guess I was a willing accomplice in a variety of scrapes she got us into. When we were quite young, she informed me one day, that if we had measles we wouldn't have to go to school. I'm actually not that sure, on reflection, I was old enough to go to school anyway, but clearly, she was. What she was saying though, did make sense and we'd both had measles before. In fact, that was the first part of the problem, we'd had measles already. She explained to me that using her painting set we'd paint measles on each other and then we'd be able to stay at home. I clearly agreed to this and I guess, early the following day and quite naked, the painting of measles spots began. My sister was clearly in a hurry as not too many spots got painted by her, on me, before she was demanding I started painting spots on her. I remember putting up a protest about this but for whatever reason I took up the brush. I soon realised it was more difficult than I expected to paint small measles spots and I was quite determined to make each spot quite round. One spot ended up being particularly large and even then, it was far from perfect. Soon after this, my sister decided the job was done and she scurried off to present herself to Mum (possibly taking me with her, I don't recall) and announcing that we had measles. Clearly Mum wasn't as easily fooled as we supposed she would be and we soon found ourselves in the bath getting the measles spots washed off.

Going to work with Dad

My Dad was a milkman and from a very early age either my sister or I would be allowed to go to work with him, in the school holidays. His job required him to leave the house as early as 4.30 or 5.00 in the morning depending on what round he was working (he was a relief milkman and covered 4 different rounds). One day my sister decided that we'd both be able to go with him if we hid in the family car and then got out to surprise him when he arrived at work. I can't recall if this was a school day or not but do remember that she would do all the planning. She had a watch and so would wake me up at an appropriate time, and we'd get dressed, unlock the back door of the house and unlock the car door. I'm not sure how she managed to unlock the car door but vaguely recollect the keys would hang on a hook underneath one of the kitchen cupboards.

Sure enough, in the middle of the night, I was woken by my sister and before long we were in the back of the car waiting for him to arrive and unwittingly take us to work. After a while we found that we were bored and so my sister decided it would be a good idea if we could listen to her radio and leaving me in the car, she went to fetch it. She was gone absolutely ages but then instead of her opening the car door with the long-awaited radio, it was instead opened by my irate Mother. It turned out my sister had got caught getting the radio but hadn't told my parents that I was in the car and only later when they decided to check whether or not I was in bed was the full scale of my sister's cunning plan discovered and thus thwarted.

Helping Dad on the Milk round

As a young kid, my Dad was a milkman and rather than having his own road he worked relief for four rounds which we called: Castor, Town, Westwood and one I can't recall. The town round was the last one he used a milk cart pulled by a horse (in the late 1960s), while mine and my sister's favourite was Castor.

The most interesting thing about the Castor round was a large park called 'Milton Park' and I was always amazed how my Dad never got lost in the park. Entry into it was by a cattle grid and reason there were lots of cattle grids in the park. There were also lots of squirrels, even some red ones at that time I believe. The roads in the park were single carriageway with some passing places. I can't remember if there were sheep in the park or not but certainly there were cows.

One morning I was helping dad on the Castor round and we were in Milton Park. This round used an electric milk float for the deliveries which on level ground had a top speed of about 20-25mph. But going down the steep Castor hill it was possible to 'pin it' and to exceed the maximum calibration of the speedo of 50 mph. So, there we were doing 20 mph in an electric milk float on the single-track road in Milton Park. Up ahead a cow was on the road. I looked at Dad wondering how he was going to get the cow to move but he did nothing. We approached the cow still at 20 mph and the cow didn't move. I got scared and shouted at Dad 'we'll hit it' but he ignored me. I looked ahead at the cow, and the cow looked at us, and in a fraction of a second before a likely impact, it jumped clear of the road. Dad looked at me and he was grinning from to ear and then chuckled. I never found out whether he'd had similar experiences with cows, or knew from his (mostly arable!) farming experience that the cow would move, or whether this was a first-time experience of a calling the cow's bluff. Either way I was impressed because if I'd have been at the wheel (and sometimes even as a kid he'd let me drive) I'd have stopped.

The mower

My Dad was a keen gardener who worked hard to keep his garden tidy with well-trimmed lawns and raised flower beds. The lawns were trimmed by a 2-stroke petrol Atco lawnmower, though I vaguely remember before that he had a push mower. As a kid, I loved all things mechanical and was particularly interested in the mower which while silenced, was about as noisy as a typical motorbike. I was allowed to watch and learn the starting routine of the mower being: petrol tap on, close choke, kick start, open hand throttle and open hand clutch. Once the lawn had been cut with my following behind Dad and the mower for the duration, he switched off the petrol tap. However, since the carburettor still had petrol in it he ran the engine until the carburettor float bowl ran dry to prevent a gradual drip of petrol on the grass or the shed floor before he put it away.

At some point in my childhood (maybe 6-10 years old), I was allowed to 'drive' the mower, under careful supervision. I was only allowed to use a light throttle opening and generally found the mower didn't steer as well when I was at the handles 'driving' as it did when he was. Still, I enjoyed these supervised 'drives'. On one occasion Dad was distracted by some other pressing task when I was about to 'drive' and as it turned out, unwisely, allowed me to 'drive' the mower wholly unsupervised. I watched him disappear to whatever task he was going to attend to before opening the throttle as wide as I dared. The engine roared and I deftly let out the clutch.

Unfortunately, being still just a young kid, I hadn't thought through the consequences of these actions and so was taken by surprise when the mower lurched forward and rapidly gathered speed. I panicked as clearly the mower was out of control and all I could do was to hang on to the handles and desperately tried to dig my heels into the grass to hold it back. The mower wasn't going to be restrained and within seconds crashed into a raised flower bed and the engine stalled. The excitement was over as quick as it had started and by this time my Dad had returned. I suppose he must have asked me for some kind of explanation which I gave to him, as I recall he did comment that he'd heard the engine rev loudly and wondered what was happening. No harm was done to either the mower (possibly the grass box had already been removed) or the flower bed and I was relieved to have survived this scary incident and without even being told off.

Central heating and the wardrobe

When we moved into a Council house in Elmfield Road, Peterborough, it didn't have central heating. So, my parents decided to have it installed. The system they chose was a solid fuel Parkray enclosed fire (with a glass door) and back boiler, just before North Sea gas heralded the arrival of cleaner and probably cheaper forms of central heating. I was probably pre-school age and found it very interesting to see all the work being done in the house over a period of many days which included a lot of pipework, fitting radiators to walls and so on. At one point my own clothes wardrobe was lain on its side for some reason, in my parents' bedroom, and the whole house was in disarray. I remember finding one of the workman's tools, I think it was a saw, and gently sawed at a loose edge of rolled up carpet. The workman who had been friendly enough until then, told me off for doing this but without even raising his voice. I wasn't pleased about being told off and my usual response was to have a sulk (it's possibly my wife would maintain that little has changed in my character over the years).

To have a proper sulk it's also necessary to go somewhere, and where better than my own wardrobe. So, while it was lying on the floor, much like a coffin, and full of my clothes, I opened the door and got inside it. Sometime later I got out again and the unfortunate workman was very relieved to see me and asked me where I'd been, though I don't think I replied. None of this seems particularly extraordinary until many years later I learned that on that occasion I had in fact been missing for some time and everyone, including more than one workman had been searching for me. I don't know how long I'd been missing for, but since it was both dark and comfortable in the wardrobe and my being of such a young age, I'd probably fallen asleep and had an afternoon nap!

The school telephone

For some reason when I was about nine years old, I was specially selected to wait outside the headmaster's office for a parcel, a message or some other such 'trusty' task that I've since forgotten what it was. In fact, I was forgotten about myself while supposedly waiting for the task and spent virtually all afternoon outside the headmaster's office (who was out). I didn't mind being forgotten that much but I could hardly day dream as his phone kept ringing. I thought about answering it but wasn't sure if I was supposed to or not. I got to think about this a lot because not long after it had stopped ringing, it started again. This seemed to go on all afternoon causing me to agonise at regular intervals what to do. Eventually I got sick and tired of the phone ringing so I entered the headmaster's office and answered it. The caller was a teacher from an Annexe of the school, Mrs Lawrence, who very surprised when I answered the phone and asked me a couple of questions. She seemed pleased as well as surprised, which was a relief as to a 9-year-old boy she was a fierce dragon and not one of the friendlier teachers in my experience. After that I forgot she'd even rang. I, myself, was remembered after that, services no longer required after all, etc, and I can't remember if I even related that the phone had rung. So, I returned to class and forgot all about it.

The next morning at school assembly (we had one every morning) the headmaster related a story that if a telephone was ringing most children would ignore it for all sorts of reasons but yesterday one very good boy was brave enough to answer the headmaster's phone. I was then named and asked to stand up and everyone had to clap. Wow, I felt my cheeks burn red, not because of the applause but because I felt such a fraud. Clearly Mrs Lawrence had neglected to mention how many times she'd rung the headmaster's phone before it got answered.

The price of admission

My parents never had much money when I was a child growing up, but this never seemed to be an obstacle to my Dad achieving something he set out to do. Credit cards hadn't yet been 'invented', or at least were unavailable to Dad. Consequently, he had to find a way to either get some extra income (he occasionally bought and sold things), or find a way to save money (he grew his own fruit and veg). At other times he had to find an alternative way around the problem of not having enough money.

Living in Peterborough also meant living a short drive from the East of England Showground which hosted various interesting events for my Dad, but less so the family. There were exceptions however, one of which was the Expo Steam Traction Engine rally. I believe there were two occasions when Dad took us to an event at the East of England Showground. The entrance was reached after driving across a narrow road or sometimes across a grassy field. There would be a series of places where you paid someone, and then you proceeded to park in a field. There would have been an age below which admission was free, probably age five. Here are a couple of instances of our admission.

Just before we pulled up to the pay point in our car, Dad suggested to my younger brother that he might like to hide under our travel rug for a while. My sister and I didn't really think anything of this and neither did my brother who willingly obliged. However, just as my Dad was paying for our admission my brother appeared from under the travel rug like a jack-in-the-box and asked my Dad 'can I come out now?' I can't remember if my Dad had to pay for the admission price of my brother or not, or if he got away with it!

Another time when we reached the paying point in our car, the person taking the admission money asked my Dad how old my younger brother was. My Dad never seemed to know how old any of us where at any given time so I guessed he may have checked with our Mum, before replying 'five'. I guess my brother was listening before calling out 'no I'm not, I'm seven'.

Dad always took these setbacks in his stride and for one of these incidences simply laughed at having been caught, and passed comment that you could never trust your kids they'd always let you down.

The light fitting in the lounge

Once at our home in Elmfield Road, and just before it was time to go to school, I was having a duffle bag fight with Philip, my younger (by 5 years) brother. It was nothing special and there was nothing particularly heavy in our bags that would have hurt each other. At one point, I managed this spectacular over the top shot that didn't hit him, as I'd intended but hit the lounge lampshade sending it swaying from side to side. This stopped me dead in my tracks but didn't stop Philip. He quickly ran to the light switch announcing that it 'had to be tested'. I didn't have time to tell him not to test it but did have long enough for a thought to pass that I'd rather he didn't. The next thing that happened took me by surprise. There was a large flash of red/orange and a very small puff of smoke that was followed by the lamp shade gently floating down to the lounge floor! I can't remember whether Mum found it, or we told her, but do recall our telling her that when we switched the light on it just happened. The house was a council house so the council would fix it. So by the end of that same day, a new ceiling rose wire and lamp fitting was in place and nothing more was said about it.

Mum says the wrong word

As a kid in the 1970s most of the swearing in our house was done by my Dad and very occasionally by my Mum. I don't think either my older sister or younger brother or myself ever swore in my parents' presence. Of course, we swore at lot at school and had a full foul-mouth vocabulary.

One-day Mum, Dad, myself and my younger brother were in the lounge. He was mucking about with something or other and it clearly irritated my Mum. So, she said to him. "Pack that in you silly twat". He immediately stopped, shocked at Mum having sworn. I stopped shocked that Mum had sworn and looked at him. Dad stopped what he was doing and looked at Mum and then he asked her "do you know what that word means?" Her reply was that it's the same as a twit only they (meaning my brother and I) muddle the letters round. His fairly formal response was "no it doesn't, I'll tell you what it means later". And from that day onwards this became one of the legendary family stories we never grew tired of telling, though I think in later years Mum denied it ever happened.

Sherry Trifle

My Dad never drank much alcohol and only occasionally drank whisky, rum in coffee (in the winter), and sherry at Christmas. He also quite liked sherry trifle and so Mum used to make the occasional sherry trifle for him though we all ate it. When I was at the young adolescent age when drinking alcohol was cool and we had a bottle of sherry in the house I would take the occasional swig from the bottle when no-one was about and liked the taste. I did however, have no idea how much sherry was meant to go in a sherry trifle and I guess my Mum didn't either and that it was simply guess work.

This is the story though of one particular sherry trifle Mum made. This trifle was partly made in that the liquid fruit base and trifle sponges were in the bowl and waiting for the jelly, custard and cream layers to go on top. For some reason, there was a lengthy transition between these layers and when no-one was looking, I decided the sherry trifle would be improved by my adding in some extra sherry. I don't know how much went in but probably it was at least as much as, if not more than, Mum originally made it with. By strange co-incidence I was in the kitchen when Dad had a look at the trifle. He grinned and said let's put some more sherry in it" and then he did. I'm certain he didn't know I'd already added extra sherry and his grin was because I guess he found it amusing to have more sherry in the trifle. I couldn't confess to already having added extra sherry as I'd be in big trouble, so said nothing and tried to look innocent. A stranger thing happened even later as I happened to be in the kitchen when Mum came in and looked at the trifle. She then said "I'm not sure there's enough sherry in this" and poured some more from the bottle into it. I don't think I told her Dad had already added some and I certainly didn't confess I'd added sherry but smiled and looked innocent. I can't say as I can remember ever eating any of the trifle and whether this was because my memory fails me or the trifle was so potent, but it's certain I did and that it was probably the strongest sherry trifle ever!

The parents evening

At my senior school, some of the pupils were required to assist at parents' evenings and myself and a friend, Kelvin, probably teenagers at this time, were duly selected or volunteered. For some reason, we turned up a lot earlier than we needed to and since the school was open, we had a bit of a muck about. At the school neither of us particularly liked the deputy head teacher who was nick-named by an abbreviated form of the name of a TV cartoon character – Dep Dog. After a while it turned out that either one, or both of us, needed to break wind. Since we were near Dep Dog's office one of suggested, and the other agreed, that we would place our backsides against Dep Dog's door and fart against it, which we did. After that we left that vicinity and it was only much later that we bumped into Dep Dog. He told us that earlier that evening he'd heard a strange noise outside his office that had caused him to 'almost jump out of skin' and had we seen anything strange happen. I looked at Kelvin who had gone very pale who shook his head in denial and said that we hadn't. We made our escape and quietly discussed that when we were farting on Dep Dog's door, he was in his room the whole time and we'd been extremely lucky not to have been caught and caned.

French

One of the new things about senior school was that you got to learn, or attempt to learn, a foreign language. I can't say I was very sold on the idea of learning another language and, like much of my school experience, if only the teachers had explained the relevance of what they were trying to teach us I might have messed about less. For example, if I'd been told that French is one of the two main languages used in motorsport it would have helped motivate me. Or, if I'd been allowed to learn a few automotive words and phrase I'd have been more interested. In fairness those things didn't occur to me either so instead I used my French dictionary to look up rude words and swear words. I had the usual accomplices in this endeavour including Kelvin.

One 'find' was the French word for Bastard which was 'batard'. It also occurred to us that the pronunciation was similar to the French word for boat, being 'bateau'. Obviously, we had to test out our discovery and I think in this respect Kelvin was either braver than I was, or better at keeping a straight face, or maybe both.

The opportunity arose one lesson when one of us had to say 'bateau' for boat. I remember Kelvin clearly saying 'Batard' which does sound similar in French. The French teacher pulled a very serious face and then said: 'Non, non'. Then he said 'bateau'. I was amazed when Kelvin looked him in the eye and simply said 'Batard' again. The French teacher again corrected what he must have assumed was a pronunciation error rather than deliberate use of a wrong word. I believe that Kelvin really stuck his neck out and said 'Batard' one more before falling into line and saying bateau.

That lesson wasn't a one off because a small group of us persisted in using 'batard' for 'bateau' always eliciting the serious 'non, non' from the teacher. I'm not certain, but I think our fun stopped because he dropped 'boat' from the verbal vocabulary part of our lessons.

The Racing Car valve

As a kid, my Dad found me a Saturday job at a classic Jaguar restoration company that happened to be next to his place of work's storage depot, on an industrial estate, in Peterborough. It was never well-paid work but mostly it was interesting. Not everyone at the company had much patience for a 12-13-14 year old kid, but one person did, and I remain grateful to him. His name was Alan Mills and he was the machinist. He had a metalworking lathe and a horizontal mill, but mostly he worked on the lathe. Not only would he find jobs for me to do he also explained things to me especially before giving me a job to do. One job I regularly undertook was the strip down of an XK 6-cyl engine cylinder head. I had to remove the cams, cam buckets, shims and then compress and remove the valves. The bare head would then be examined and often as not repairs made to corrosion on the water ways and other cleaning up undertaken before it was sent away to be skimmed. When it returned, Alan rebuilt the head as required, sometimes with an upgrade to larger than standard valves along with some porting and occasionally replacement of valve guides. Most heads however, were rebuilt with standard valves and one of my jobs was to clean the 6 inlet and 6 exhaust valves.

When, I first took on this task there was a large stockpile of used valves to be cleaned. It wasn't a bad job albeit a bit repetitive and dirty. I put the valve to be cleaned in the chuck of a pillar drill and firstly scraped off the heavy carbon deposits with a broken industrial size hacksaw blade that was provided for this task, complete with insulating tape wrapped around one end to act as the handle. With the worst of the carbon removed, next I used some emery cloth to polish the valve. Finally, the valve was removed from the drill and placed in a container along with all the other cleaned valves. When a cylinder head was being rebuilt, a used valve was selected by Alan and after checking it wasn't bent, he refaced the valve and then lapped it into the cylinder head.

As an indulgence, the company owned and raced a classic Jaguar XK120 and the engine was regularly rebuilt either for some sort of upgrade, or after a catastrophic failure of which at one time there were several.

One of the partners of the company would on occasion lose his temper and I was always careful to keep out of his way generally, as much as possible. He was ok with me but he never valued any of the work I did or recognised that I was reasonably capable for a range of tasks. I remember on one occasion the racing car cylinder head was being re-fitted to the engine with the engine still in the car. Everyone was helping and I helped too, by placing D shaped washers on the head studs. I noted some studs had been randomly orientated but made sure mine were correctly orientated with the flat side of the D against the flat wall of the head. I was politely told 'no disrespect son but this is too important to let you do this' or words to that effect. The 'no disrespect' had exactly the opposite meaning, so I wandered off without commenting that while not all the washers were correctly fitted, mine certainly were. And that's how it was – I wasn't allowed to touch the mechanical parts of the racing car. I was surprised then one day when Alan asked me to clean the racing car valves which were practically immediately required for him to re-fit to the racing car head. Alan told me to take care not to drop a valve but if I did drop one to let him know. I guessed this was because if the valve bent after being dropped, and it wasn't detected before being rebuilt, it would have been likely to cause a serious problem if not engine failure. Apart from the obvious reason of giving me this instruction I couldn't really see why he'd told me because I don't think I had ever dropped a single valve out of the hundreds I'd cleaned. Each valve was going back to the same combustion chamber it had been removed from and there would have been a piece of wood or cardboard marked with the chamber number to prevent any mix-ups.

The racing car's valves differed from the valves I'd normally cleaned up in several respects. Firstly, especially the inlets, were much larger than standard valves. In fact, the racing car inlet valves were larger than D-type racing valves and larger than any large valves fitted to customers big valve racing heads. They also had hardly any carbon on them but had some sticky, rather than dry, deposits. I'm guessing now that the sticky residue was due to the large amount of STP added to the engine oil and also because more of that oil than should have done, ran down the valve guides. I remember thinking the valves needed cleaning more with solvent than emery paper not least because I could see a shiny sparkling dust of metal being removed from the valve more than carbon dust as I applied the emery cloth. I thought this was a pity because the valves as well as being very large and of a flatter shape than regular valves, had a yellow tinted chrome-like polished finish to them rather than dull metal grey of regular valves.

Then it happened! I dropped an inlet valve onto the floor. I carefully picked it up and it looked Ok to my untrained eye. I remembered what Alan had told me and considered it against my childhood experiences and similar comments made to me by my parents. I'd learnt from an early age that owning up to an accident or mistake to my parents resulted in anger and harsh punishment such that it was better not to admit to anything, hope it wouldn't be discovered and it if was then lie. For example, if my parents said 'tell us the truth and you won't get smacked' I'd found that in fact telling the truth did result in getting a smack! However, Alan wasn't my parent, in fact I don't think he had children of his own and had always been patient and kind to me. So, with some trepidation I told him I'd dropped a valve and which one it was. I don't recall him showing an emotion of any kind, but he simply checked the valve, then told me it was ok (not bent) and never mentioned it again. Nor did my dropping the racing car valve ever change anything and I worked for him after that as if it had never happened. He was a great guy and always good to work for.

Fireworks in Peterborough

In the 1970s, you had to be sixteen years old to be able to legally buy fireworks and in 1979 I was, and so were some of my school friends. One day we'd been to Peterborough 'tech' college where we studied Accounts and Economics, two subjects school offered but that you had to go to 'tech' to study. There was a short-cut back from the 'tech' to where most of us lived and one day it just so happened to be that time of year when fireworks were on sale in the shops. Kevin Fletcher (also known as Fletch) had some bangers he'd purchased and rather than let one off in the conventional manner someone suggested he do a 'genie'. None of us had done a 'genie' before but the idea was that by emptying the gunpowder from the banger and lighting it, a large puff of smoke was produced like an old Hollywood film that announced the arrival of a 'genie'. Fletch found a suitable spot for making the 'genie' and emptied out the gunpowder from the banger. Then at absolute arm's length he lit a match and flicked it on the gunpowder.

Nothing. He tried again and again, gradually getting nearer and nearer and still nothing. Somebody, it might have been me, suggested we empty the fuse part of the banger onto the main pile of gunpowder. I remember when he did this noticing this powder was both a lighter colour and finer grain than the main pile. Fletch struck another match and having long since given up his arm's length approach practically had his head over the pile of gunpowder. POOOF, there was a short orange flash and a large cloud of smoke that completely enveloped Fletch. So, success at last and after getting over our initial surprise how we laughed and laughed.

Quality Street sweets at Christmas

Even as kids growing up, Dad had bad teeth. What's more as a result of some real 'butchering' by a dentist in his own childhood, he no longer went to a dentist. Consequently, he couldn't eat toffee sweets but liked the occasional chocolate, especially soft centres. One year my parents made the mistake of buying a tin of 'Quality Sweet' sweets, long before Christmas. While on the annual present hunt (in my parents' wardrobe or on top of it were obvious hiding places) my brother and I discovered the 'Quality Sweet' tin. I had the bright idea of very carefully opening the seal under the tin and easing out a sweet or two for myself and my brother. I think the coffee soft centres went first, followed by all the other tastier sweets in the tin. I guess over the weeks leading up to Christmas the tin was gradually depleted and despite my giving the tin a shake to unsettle the contents by Christmas it was probably half a tin when Dad opened it. He was quickly unimpressed by what seemed to him to be less than a full tin, and he soon got very angry when he found most of the sweets were toffees which he couldn't eat. He went on about this for some time and in between swearing and stating what he thought about 'Quality Street' he even talked about writing a letter of complaint to the manufacturer. My brother and I realised a confession wouldn't be any good so we just kept quiet and said nothing. Sorry Dad.

The writing competition

Dad always had untidy handwriting and probably he was the only person who could actually read it. He also had arthritic hands which didn't help. Dad could also play his cards close to his chest and planned for all sorts of things that only came to light once he'd done them. It seemed to come out of the blue that Dad decided he was going to learn to type, in fact touch type, which in the mid-1970s wasn't the sort of thing anyone else's Dad was taking up. Dad went off to college once a week and always came home quite cheerful without providing any detail of anyone else learning to type at the college except that they were all young and female. In due course Dad passed the RSA typing course and had by this time purchased a manual typewriter and revealed the master plan was to write a gardening column for one of the local newspapers and in this he succeeded.

Typing didn't improve Dad's handwriting and he typed nearly everything on his typewriter, even quite short notes. Then, one day the local newspaper had a competition which to win you had to decipher some really bad handwriting. We all laughed and made fun of Dad for entering but he had the last laugh because he won! A man from the newspaper came around with Dad's prize which was a Smiths Corona electric typewriter. The man explained that if Dad didn't want it they'd buy it off him as the ladies in his office didn't have a typewriter as good as the one Dad won. However, he did want it, and from that point forward he typed all his gardening columns on it. In the late 1970s Dad upgraded to one of the very early Amstrad computers and he either gave me his electric typewriter or I bought it from him. So, from typing up Dad's gardening columns the Smith Corona electric typewriter was used by me when I first started writing my car magazine features.

Who's that?

After leaving school my first job was as an apprentice car welder and panel-beater, despite having more aptitude and knowledge for mechanics. Welding and panel-beating was apparently a better paid and more highly skilled job, though in my short experience it certainly wasn't well paid. I got the job with some help from my Dad whose niece's boyfriend at that time, was a paint sprayer at a local car body-shop whose Dad happened to own it. I can't remember how long it was after I'd been working there, but one day I purchased some metal segs (segments of metal). These segs were also known by the brand name of 'Blakeys' which were flat, but embossed, metal half-moon pieces of metal fitted to the heel of a shoe or boot, in my case my working boots. The idea of the Blakey was to extend the life of the heel section of the boot, the metal being harder wearing than rubber. It was also possible to strike sparks by using a sharp flicking motion of the boot heel against a suitable hard abrasive surface like a paving slab. Not least you made a tap-tap or click-click noise when you walked. I didn't think anything of it at the time, but by coincidence the manager and owner of the company had metal segs in his shoes.

The workplace building was divided into different sections with doors in between them such that if entering the paint-shop from the body-shop it was necessary to go through a door. It wasn't very long before I noticed something odd happened when I went into the paint shop. I had the vague impression that just as I passed through the door the two paint sprayers jumped and then stopped and laughed. It seems they'd been lounging around and mistook my tap-tap as being the arrival of the boss. It wasn't look before I had a similar experience after I'd been in the paint shop and went into the body shop where the other apprentice likewise jumped into action when I came through the door. This happened quite regularly for a few days though the paint sprayers thought I walked slightly faster than the boss but even so it wasn't look before I was 'encouraged' to remove the segs.

The Market Drayton 'Moped Mafia'

When Yamaha introduced the world's fastest production 250cc motorbike in the form of the RD250LC (the previous quickest was the Suzuki X7) I decided to get one. By the time I did get one a new colour scheme was available being Black with red and orange highlights so this was the model I purchased. Eventually I took and passed my motorcycle test which meant that not only could I write my 250cc motorbike without learner plates I could also have a pillion passenger.

Market Drayton, where the family moved to in 1979 from Peterborough, had at that time a small market square where occasionally anyone with a motorbike might meet other bikers. More often than not though, it would be where 16-year-old youths with 50cc Mopeds, known as the 'moped mafia' would 'hang out' of an evening. One evening I was in the square at the same time as the 'moped mafia' with fuel in my motorbike's tank, time on my hands and not much happening. One of the older looking youths looked at me and with a fairly unhopeful looking expression asked 'I don't suppose you'll take me for a ride on the back' or words to that effect. I rarely took a pillion passenger on my motorbike but since he'd asked and I had nothing else to do I agreed.

The obvious 'round trip' was to the bypass, flat out down the bypass and back to the market square. The unknown pillion passenger jumped on the back and I set off in an appropriately impressive manner. Once on the bypass I accelerated to maximum speed and got flat on the tank. As the speed was building towards maximum, I became aware of an unexpected problem. Up ahead there were some road works with traffic lights. I decided that I could just about get the bike to 'top out' before braking for the lights and as soon as I did so I braked hard. The second problem was that I'd made my judgement on the stopping distance with just myself on the bike, rather than with a passenger. As I braked as hard as I could and watch the lights looming up on red the bike eventually stopped with a slight judder. I was relieved I'd been able to stop in time and had forgotten about the passenger but he soon made his presence felt.

'Wow, how fast was that, how fast was that' he wanted to know. I was still recovering from the unexpected stop and casually announced the speed to him with which he was delighted, probably being the fastest he'd been at that time. Once back at the Market Square he profusely thanked me to which I casually accepted, having travelled at similar speeds virtually every time I'd ridden the bike and then rode to do nothing else in particular. I'd have forgotten about this experience except that every now and then I'd be riding my bike through town and a moped rider would be frantically flashing their headlights and putting up a hand which I always acknowledged. I realised that this moped rider was the pillion passenger and that the pillion ride on my Yamaha RD250LC had made him very happy.

Save a prayer

I moved with the family from Peterborough to Market Drayton Shropshire in the December before the June when I sat my GCE O-level exams. I never really had time to make firm friends at my new school, though before long I'd see faces of people, I'd recognised from being at school, when out drinking or partying. One such person was Richard Ford. I think his parents owned a local shop and he had a younger sister, Emma. Richard was the original genuine nice guy, well spoken, never angry and never saying bad things about other people, even if they merited it. In lots of ways he was the opposite to myself. He had a girlfriend who may have come from Luton or maybe Reading. He also drove a customised Volkswagen Beatle. I think the engine was mildly tuned and oversized at about 1600cc compared to normal Beatle engines of 1300cc. It was a dark metallic blue and may have had Wolfrace slot alloy wheels and a chrome chain steering wheel. It would have been sometime early in 1982 that he ended up working at some place as myself in Telford. I generally caught a works' bus service, or at that time may have used my motorbike. There were a few occasions though when Richard gave me a lift to work, though maybe later he also switched to using the bus.

One thing I remember very clearly is that the first thing he said whenever I got in his car (it was the backseat because the front was already taken) was 'have you got your seat belt on'. Then, once you'd replied that you had, he'd say hello, good morning or whatever.

One icy December evening Richard and some friends had apparently gone to a party or nightclub in nearby Shrewsbury. He'd left his car parked in town. Sadly, in the early hours of the next morning 18 December 1982 he died in a car accident, aged eighteen years old. From what I can recall, either hearing it at the time, or maybe I read a coroners or police report in the newspaper, he was the driver of the friend's car returning back to Market Drayton. However, he felt tired on the drive back so had stopped the car and moved to a passenger seat (front I guess) and someone else took over the driving. Then on a treacherous bend on a road that hadn't been gritted there was a patch of ice and the car left the road and crashed. It seems Richard had ironically and fatally, forgotten to fasten his seat belt and was thrown out of the car and killed.

His was the first funeral I ever attended and the church was packed, as you'd expect for a kind, caring and popular young man. I think he helped a local band, Triple Echo, as a 'roadie' and at the church they played 'Save a prayer' which was a popular song of that time by Duran Duran. I've never forgotten his cheery smile or that in his car that smile never appeared until you had your seat-belt fastened.

On the service sheet for his memorial service these words were written *'...when you are sorrowful look again into your heart and you shall see that in truth you are weeping for that which has been your delight.'* Less than five years later I used the same words on the service sheet for my own Father's memorial service. Unlike Richard I survived the major car crashes of my youth but I was conscious and sometimes reminded that he hadn't. I wish I'd got to know him better before he died.

Leather trousers

As a young lad of eighteen years old while having a healthy interest in women I never spent any time trying to learn about them and understand them, nor set out impress them. I guess the reason for this was that I more interested in cars and even at that age I didn't make huge efforts in learning about cars but did spent lots of money, later on, making them look impressive (to the un-trained eye).

I was a Clerical Assistant (CA) in the Civil Service, this being lowest grade, and worked in an office of at least thirty people. There was a supervisor grade above the CAs, a manager above that and a manager of the manager. Both the managers had their own small offices, we all worked in an open plan office. The office environment was formal, and it was unwritten rule, especially for youngsters like me, to address the managers at Mrs whatever.

Not long after getting a motorbike and after crashing it on black ice on the way to work one morning, which left me with a scar on my waist, I purchased some black leather trousers. They were purchased from a motorbike shop but weren't thick and padded biker trousers, more like regular leather trousers. On reflection, as I type this, I suppose they might even have been designed for a woman being a twenty-eight-inch waist size and while fitted me ok, were tight.

On the days I rode my motorbike to work I wore the leather trousers. It took my supervisor to point out to me that wherever I went there was at least one woman who stopped to stare at me, or rather the trousers. Being young and naïve I never really thought much of this or used it to any advantage. There was one incident though that underlines this.

The manager's manager stopped by my desk one day, and I if remember correctly, actually bent down on her knees and ran her leg over the top of my thigh and knee. She then asked either who got to polish the trousers or did my girlfriend polish them. I replied, being somewhat surprised to be asked, that I polished them myself. She got up from her knees (assuming she'd been on them) and laughed and said 'that's not much fun' and left. How strange I thought.

A Late-night mistake

Shortly after an unscheduled barrel roll in my Mini resulting in it being virtually a total financial loss (on third party insurance) I bought a Mk3 2000GT Ford Cortina and had a bank loan at least twice its value to show for it. It was a good car and served me well. I did feel a bit sorry for my Dad though, when he realised, I'd purchased a cheap second-hand car that was the same age as his Austin Maxi and with very comparable mileage (though he bought the Maxi when it was six months old).

Despite its two-litre engine and GT badge the Cortina was never quick and it was only decades later that I understood not only why, but what I could have done it about it. Also, at that time, I don't think even the current Ford Sierra was fitted with a five-speed gearbox and certainly the Cortina had just a four-speed box.

Although the driveway of the family home was long enough for three cars and room for a car in the garage, it sometimes worked out that I needed to park my car in the garage of an evening as Dad would be first out the next day. Or on a weekend I might come home late and park behind Dad's car and then if he needed to go out first one of us would have to move my car. Dad's solution was to modify the front lawn so I could get the Cortina parked on it at an angle. So rather than turn ninety degrees into our drive to park I simply needed to slow down and turn maybe forty-five degrees to park it.

After a night out, assuming I was the designated non-drinking driver for the evening, returning home, I'd have to change down to first gear to turn into our road (which being a close, was a dead-end). Then I'd put my throttle foot to the floor, grab second gear, and then brake and turn into the special parking slot Dad had made for me. This would usually be the early hours of the morning, though the Cortina wasn't particularly noisy so never an issue.

One night I must have managed a slightly higher speed turning into our road, got into second gear earlier than usual and decided I could grab third gear and then brake. This turned out to be a late-night mistake! I found I was going much quicker than usual and was unlikely to slow down in time to park. It would have been sensible to brake further down the road, turn around at the bottom and then park. What I actually did though was simply brake much harder than usual which locked the wheels and caused the tyres to screech as the car skidded down the road. Just as I got near our house, I took my foot off the brakes, did a gentle swerve and parked no more than a foot to the side of where I should have been. I also deftly switched the lights off and laid low across the front seats. I was aware that two or maybe three or more houses in the street now had a bedroom light switched on, but they wouldn't be able to tell it was me. After waiting for the lights to go out, I got out of the car, locked it, and went into the house. I guess the skid marks down the street told a story in the morning but those marks didn't finish on our driveway!

A trip to the Cottage Hospital

Market Drayton was a small town and unlike Peterborough where we had moved from, didn't have an Accident and emergency (A&E) Hospital. What it did have was what was called at that time, a Cottage Hospital. Since I was five years older than my brother, while he was at school I'd left, got a job and owned a car (and a motorbike before that). One day the car came in useful. This was the day my brother came rushing through the rear gate of our house and threw his bike to the ground and was in some pain. I learned that he'd hurt his hand having just been in a fight. It was possible he'd broken a bone in his hand and it could see it was swelling up so without telling my parents any of this detail I told them we were both going out and then I drove him to the cottage hospital.

We'd agreed that Mum and Dad didn't need to know anything about the fight and went inside the hospital. We were met almost at once by the duty nurse who gave us a very charming smile because she knew us both very well since she was our Auntie Janet! We had forgotten she worked at the hospital and I expect she saw the look of awkward surprise on our faces. We had to concoct some sort of explanation about how the 'accident' had happened on the spot, and I guess we weren't very convincing as she smiled even more as we spoke. It did occur to us at the time that she might not have been fooled but decided we'd stick to the same story to tell our parents and probably the story was that he'd crashed his bike. She did a very nice job of bandaging his hand, having ascertained it wasn't broken but badly bruised and either confirmed our story to our parents or said nothing because they simply accepted when we told them (they didn't smile knowingly) our concocted story to explain the bandage. Unlike us though, they weren't surprised that Auntie Janet was the duty nurse.

Unwashed at Breakfast

As a teenager going on twenty years of age living in Market Drayton Shropshire I liked to party on a Friday and Saturday night. Of course, I was never actually invited to any parties any more than my friends were, we were gate crashers. We'd be in the pub and over hear people talking about a party and if we didn't also overhear the address, we'd discreetly follow them. The upshot of all this is that I'd drink an excessive amount of alcohol and when I woke up the following morning, I'd be slightly dehydrated (a side effect of drinking alcohol) and I'd be thirsty.

Waking up thirsty also meant that unlike now, when I clean my teeth and have a wash before going downstairs, then I simply went downstairs straight after getting out of bed for a mug of tea or coffee. I don't always bother having breakfast on a weekend and on the particular instance of this story I can't recall if I did or didn't. In fact, I can't even recall if there was a small breakfast table in the kitchen of that house or not, maybe there was, along with a couple of stools.

The thing I do remember clearly on one occasion, was my Mum giving me a beady eyed look. She almost never looked at me like this and so it was immediately obvious to me. I found this slightly disconcerting but given a bowl of cereal and a mug of tea/coffee doesn't take long to consume, I didn't have to bear her scrutiny for long, and I was back upstairs for a wash (and to probably clean my teeth – generally they were neglected now to my everlasting regret).

There it was, in full view in the mirror. The explanation for the beady eyed scrutiny of my Mum! A faint imprint of lipstick on my check, red/pink if I remember correctly. It had survived the night and remained as a witness in the morning. My Mum never mentioned this but I can imagine that after the beady eyed look she would have reached the thought: 'that boy's got lipstick on his cheek'.

The Lombard RAC Rally

In Market Drayton, I used to catch a 'work's bus to work under at that time what was a Civil Service initiative called an 'Assisted Travel Scheme'. Ironically this took longer, and was more expensive, than subsequent private contract with the very same coach company (which was a later 'development'). One of the guys on the bus was named Alan Cartwright and one day he asked me and several other colleagues if we wanted to marshal on the RAC rally. I readily agreed and so began an annual adventure over a number of years to which I remain very grateful to Alan for.

One year we were going to marshal just outside the special stage of the Clocaenog Forest. I'd learned that rally cars drive on the public highway obeying all speed limits etc and then drive flat out on closed sections of forest track, stately homes or racetracks. Our job was simply to point the cars into the direction of the special stage while they were still on the public highway, so I was a bit disappointed that while we'd see all the cars they wouldn't be travelling at speed. However, Clocaenog was a night stage and were on 'duty' from just about midnight through to the early hours of the morning. It was a fairly uneventful night and as the early hours of the morning wore on the cars became less frequent and it was only the occasional straggler that appeared that we pointed in the right direction. Then after we'd neither seen nor heard a car for some time we heard a very sick sounding car that was dragging a broken exhaust at a fairly slow speed. The car, which was a Lotus Sunbeam with a French driver and navigator wound down a window, and showing me a rally road book for the first time in my life, asked for directions to Ju day ga lo. I spoke neither French or Welsh and Judaygalo was a place I'd never heard of. A colleague, possibly Alan himself quickly established they wanted Dollgellau which was a service halt and where the French car could be fixed and so pointed them in the right direction. He explained they didn't have much hope of completing the rally as they would be out of road time. And so, we thought nothing more about this and looked ahead to when we'd officially be stood down.

Much later that morning as dawn was approaching still and silent, I heard a faint noise that sounded like a car. The noise of the car increased and in the peace of the dawn, the sound carried. It was apparent that the car was in fact a rally car and that it was being driven absolutely flat out. I heard every rev change whether for a gear change, reduction or increase of speed, for a bend or straight, and it sounded great! Then it appeared in sight, it was the Lotus Sunbeam and French crew. They clearly knew which direction to take and entered the T-junction of the road where we were standing in a 'full-on' but controlled, sideways slide. As they sped past us, the navigator held up his hand in acknowledgement and as quickly as they appeared in our sight they were gone, but it made the whole night and early morning in the cold worth it.

The Lombard RAC rally and driving the stage

One of the fun things about being a marshal on the Lombard RAC rally in the early eighties was that sometimes you'd have to drive your road car through the special stage to get to where you'd be marshalling. In future years this practice was banned due to the delays caused by marshal's crashing their cars on the stage. My road car at this time was a Mk3 2000cc Ford Cortina GT which wasn't as capable as it should have been, which with knowledgeable hindsight was almost certainly due to the previous (taxi driver) owner jetting the carburettor for lean and economical running, rather than maximum power. It was a rear wheel drive car so on low grip surfaces: grass, gravel, ice, etc, a sharp application of throttle, especially in a lower gear, caused the back end of the car to step out dramatically (over-steer). This gave the car a sideways stance like a rally car, corrected with fistfuls of opposite lock and was fun to do.

However, driving down a heavily cambered and frosty forest track I actually didn't want any oversteer and I think I daren't drive any faster than about sixty plus miles per hour using third gear but with lots of light braking and moderate applications of throttle.

On another occasion, myself and several other cars including Alan Cartwright's were going to drive through a stage and park up to marshal. We were given instructions as well as some sort of marker board that I carefully place on the roof of my car, and off we went. My departure was from a grassy area so I set off with a full throttle opening, a massive sideways slide, followed by opposite lock. I'd forgotten about the marker board on the roof and it was never seen by me again. Eventually we arrived at the parking spot and Alan asked me words to the effect of 'What were you playing at'? I was surprised to be asked this as it was pretty much custom and practice to drive sideways and Alan was an easy-going guy. I replied I was doing what everyone else was doing to which Alan replied 'but you only just missed that tree'. So, in fact Alan was concerned that my driving had almost resulted in an unpleasant accident. As for the tree, well I'd never seen it.

Sleeping on the job

The second job I had, after leaving school, was as a clerical worker at a large MOD stores depot. Being MOD (Army) meant that aside from working with a bunch of other civil servants, on occasion I worked with enlisted serviceman, soldiers ranging from privates to Majors. One day our 'team' were given a private to work with us and he was a fairly lively and young Welshman who advised us his name was Taff McGrath. It's possible his first name, which I don't think he ever used, was Philip. One morning he came into work and he explained that he'd been drinking until very late and was really tired. Since our office was large and he wouldn't be obviously missed, I had the bright suggestion that he could lock himself into a toilet cubicle, put the seat down, and go to sleep. One of us would then wake him up in an hour's time. He agreed and off he went.

After an hour, I went to the gents' loo, banged on the appropriate cubicle door but nothing happened. He was seemingly fast asleep. I reported back to my colleagues whose efforts likewise confirmed he was fast asleep. As the morning wore on, we tried a number of things to get him to wake up including throwing balls of rolled up paper over the top of the cubicle. At one point, I stood on the seat in the adjacent cubicle to get a better shot with a ball of rolled paper and even a bull's eye didn't wake him up.

I could see he was sitting in a slumped position with his head to one seat. I think he may have been snoring so back with the team we agreed that we might as well simply leave him there until he woke up and nobody missed him. I think it was early afternoon when he finally pitched up back his desk, feeling fully refreshed and glad of his sleep.

The fruit packers

In nineteen eighty-four my parents moved house from Market Drayton, Shropshire to Courteenhall, Northamptonshire and I'd moved with them. I was twenty years old and I needed a job. The job only had to be temporary as I was about to enlist in the RAF in about a fortnight's time. After registering with various job agencies, I quickly found work at a fruit and vegetable packing warehouse just outside the town centre. The work did vary slightly but none of it was interesting.

One task was trimming bunches of grapes to fit into a punnet. Another was to shrink wrap an aubergine, and so on. A lot of the workforce was female and being one of the few men was perhaps why I was giving a slightly heavier manual work task on occasion.

The fruit packers purchased goods wholesale and then packed them in much smaller sizes for retail outlets such as M&S and Sainsburys. Consequently, they produced lots of packing rubbish including lots of wooden tomato boxes. The rubbish all went into special closed compacting skip that looked brand new and was painted bright blue. My job was to throw the rubbish into the skip and compact it, so some more could go in. I couldn't see the compactor at work because there was some sort of electrical interlock that prevented it working if the access doors were open. I could of course hear it and it sounded just like a council rubbish/dust cart when it was compacting. Every few days it would be taken away and emptied (possibly from a large door at the front) and then returned.

I quickly got bored throwing tomato boxes into the skip and compressing the contents every now and again. So, I hit upon the idea of stacking them into the skip so that I could get the maximum number in it before closing the doors and pressing the button that started the compactor. After the first couple of compactions I got more skilled at the stacking (all done through the access doors) and was spending longer on the stacking, trying to get as tight a stack as possible. When I finally couldn't squeeze another box into the stack and closed the doors, I pressed the button to start the compaction. The compaction started and then all of a sudden BLAM! I jumped back, releasing the button and saw that the access doors, which looked to be made of quarter inch steel plate, were buckled out. I tried to open them but the locking bolt was also jammed. I looked around and it seemed like no-one else had seen my drama. I found another job to do and forgot about the compactor. It was the next day or maybe the day after that before the compactor skip was taken away, emptied and returned. I had some boxes to crush but the access doors were still jammed. I think I left it for a day or so before telling someone the skip had been emptied but I couldn't get the doors opened and they bashed them in enough so they would open and close. After that I just threw the boxes in and didn't bother stacking them anymore.

An Aga cooker and a hairdryer

While living at Courteenhall in Northamptonshire my parents decided to go on holiday and leave my brother and myself at home. We made several jokes before they left about having wild parties but had no intention of doing so (my brother was about 16/17 years old and I'd be about 21/22 years old). We did conduct a couple of entertaining experiments, this one which I think was of my instigation.

Being a country house while having an electric cooker, it was not on mains gas, and in fact had probably not always been connected to the national grid. At least I assume that was the reason why it also had a log burning range type cooker, either an Aga or a Rayburn. While on the face of things not very exciting for something that burned wood, it did interestingly have a temperature gauge. One of us, probably myself, decided the range needed testing to see how hot we could get it.

We soon lit the fire and started to stoke it up and watched the gauge go around the dial. I had the bright idea that if we could get more air into the fire, much like a blacksmith's bellows at a forge, it would get even hotter still. Mum's hairdryer was quickly found (possibly in a kitchen drawer) and pressed into service to blow air. I had the door of the range open and the hairdryer at full chat when suddenly my brother shouted 'whoa, whoa' or similar words to that effect.

I looked to see what the fuss was about and it was apparent the back of the hairdryer while not on fire, was molten and misshapen. I suppose that rather than just blow cold air into the range it had created some sort of vortex and was pulling hot air from the range through itself first. We abandoned the hairdryer to cool down and since the kitchen was now very hot, ceased the 'experiment' and opened all the kitchen doors and windows.

After Mum and Dad returned from their holiday one of us, probably my brother as he was generally more convincing at this type of thing, explained that while using the hairdryer the back melting had 'just happened'. Since the hairdryer still worked, while remaining misshapen nothing more was said and Mum was none the wiser until she read this story more than twenty-five years later.

A visit to the dentist

Not long after moving to Courteenhall I was going to enlist in the RAF and I needed to get my teeth in order before I did so. I had a flick through the yellow pages and being a single man decided that 'Miss White' was clearly the dentist for me. As things turned out while Miss White was a very pleasant, not unattractive woman whom I suppose might be positively described as buxom, she was probably old enough to be my mother. Having neglected my teeth by a lack of brushing combined with a high intake of heavily sugared coffee from childhood I was very accustomed to having a rotten tooth filled. So, while Miss White was a new dentist to me and needed to fill a tooth, the procedure wasn't new to me.

When she asked if I wanted an injection to numb the pain of the drilling, I declined. The reason for this decision was that in my extensive experience of dental treatment (though as it turned out dentists clearly inferior to Miss White) the injection hurt more than filling did, though I suppose on reflection it would. So, the chair was lowered and Miss White proceeded to drill out my rotten tooth and I soon experienced some severe pain. I suppose I began to move about a bit on the dental couch and before I knew it Miss White had most of her body against mine! In fact, I think she pretty much had her knee on my chest with all her weight behind it. Once the drilling was finished an exasperated if not angry Miss White exclaimed that for the next filling 'I was bloody well going to have an injection'. I supposed that even a painful injection wasn't going to hurt as much as drilling was and not being in any position to argue, I let Miss White gave me an injection for the next filling. What can I say? I didn't even feel the injection let alone the drilling and I emerged from the dentist a wiser and possibly more experienced patient than I had been previously.

Wisdom Teeth

I had managed to keep my wisdom teeth despite dental advice to the contrary, long before joining the RAF. Then while at RAF Brize Norton I had tooth ache which turned out to be an inflamed gum caused by at least one of my wisdom teeth only partially breaking through the gums. I was referred to the RAF Hospital at Wroughton where I was told, or maybe recommended to me, that I'd have my wisdom teeth removed under general anaesthetic.

After a preliminary visit for x-rays and stuff I was now at Wroughton for the extraction. It just so happened that since I was too old for my Mother to check I was wearing pyjamas, I'd given up wearing them and ever since I've nearly always slept naked. However, a patient for dental extraction can't be operated on naked or wander around even in their underpants so I was issued with a pair of RAF pyjamas. I guess service issue pyjamas had been missed off uniform updates over the years and these didn't have an elasticated waistband but a proper pyjama cord, a bit like an extra thick shoe lace that you tied up in a bow. I can't remember if they also had a button as well but they were loose fitting and draughty.

After the operation when I regained consciousness, I discovered general anaesthetic didn't really agree with me and I was very sick. It was the middle of the night and infrequently a nurse would come around and check the patients, myself included, were ok. At some point, while I find it funny now, I found it less so at the time, a middle-aged nurse came to check on me.

I was sitting on the edge of the bed with a sick bowl in my hands feeling pretty awful and realised the nurse was by my side checking I was ok. Dark as it was on the ward and as sick as I was, I noticed she was looking down at something. I wondered what she was looking at and so I looked down to see if I could see what it was. Then I realised that most likely she was looking at my willy, exposed by the draughty pyjamas. I did wonder why she bothered as she must have seen lots by now in her career as a nurse and mine didn't strike me as being any more than 'average'. I felt slightly sad at being visually taken advantage of yet counterbalanced by some regret at not being able to even deliver a chat-up line since I was so ill. Then she was gone and I went back to bed.

Ascension Island – Christmas and New Year

In the mid-1980s if you were in the air force, and I was, and in the administration trade, and I was, it was a certainty that within a year or two of enlistment you'd spend four months in the Falkland Islands or six months in Ascension Island. I'm assuming Ascension Island was the longer 'tour' because it was more pleasant. For example, on Ascension Island you could spend your weekend getting a suntan on the beach.

So, I decided that rather than wait to see if my luck meant I went to Ascension rather than the Falklands, I'd volunteer for just Ascension. It wasn't an unusual request to volunteer for what was called a 'South Atlantic' tour but it was to specify just Ascension, though I can't imagine why. After my sergeant checked I could be specific in my request, and I applied, it wasn't long before I was actually there.

So, on Christmas day 1985 I was on Ascension Island and very pleased about it. The weather was nearly always warm and sunny and life was inexpensive. I'd paid my credit card down to the lowest it had been for years and while I was supposed to be studying Law at GCE A-level my reading was diverted by 'Tuning BL's A-series engine' by David Vizard. I went running every night in about eighty degrees of heat (even when the sun had gone down) and was in great shape.

I guess for the married guys, with or without children, Christmas Day on Ascension Island wasn't such a great prospect. However, one thing everyone was going to share was Christmas dinner. The RAF always have a special Christmas dinner for the airmen with the tradition being that the officers serve the airman which while on the face of it was very gracious of them it was apparently something they actually enjoyed and some RAF stations they volunteered for.

It happened that I was at the end of the airman's mess that got served their Christmas Dinner first and so had eaten most if not all of it before the trouble started. Unlike the Army where the divisions are by regiment, for the most part while there are divisions in the RAF by flying squadrons, the majority of serving personnel aren't in a flying squadron, so the divisions are diverse and sometimes by enlisted trade. Two trades that weren't overly fond of each other were air movements staff (movers) and supply (stackers). From memory the trouble started with the movers and stackers when a stuffing ball or Brussel sprout was thrown from one group to the other and then 'returned'. Within seconds everything had escalated into the most amazing food fight I've ever seen and I was in the middle of it. The scene reminded me of one of those old Hollywood films and the air was so thick with airborne food, visibility was very limited.

Along with a couple of close friends I dived under the tables and watched for a while. The 'action' was interrupted by some corporal denouncing the behaviour but he was quickly pelted down. My friends and I decided we might as well leave, while we were still laughing, and this turned out, at least to me to have a final bonus. There was one senior officer, Sqn Ldr for Admin who I'd always found a bit stuck-up and pompous and he'd decided to leave at about the same time. I could see he had an expression on his face that was a mixture of disgust and disappointment when I also saw a gravy-soaked Brussel sprout hit him on the chest, on his best uniform tropical bush jacket, leaving a brown mark behind it. Well that just about made my Christmas day, and was the best Christmas day I had for many years.

After Christmas came new year and it's worth explaining that one of the peculiarities of the Armed Forces is that there is very little socialising permitted between rank groups being: airmen, senior non-commissioned officers (NCO's), and officers. The other peculiarity is that men outnumber women virtually everywhere (the exception being forces hospitals). RAF Ascension Island was pretty much the norm though having worked in a virtually all male environment at RAF Brize Norton there were some women including two officers at Ascension in the office I worked in. One officer's name was Carol and she was ok, being neither attractive nor unattractive.

One exception to the no socialising between rank groups at Ascension Island was Christmas and New Year. Whether this was to help morale or make Christmas more cheerful wasn't something I gave a lot of thought to

A lot of people got drunk a lot of the time at Ascension Island but I'd pretty much given up drinking alcohol some years ago when I got tired of the room spinning around, being sick and feeling awful the next day. I made an exception for New Year's Eve which was possibly also the event themed as the

Shipwreck party – where you wore what you were wearing when 'the ship went down' – I wore a bath towel. (I think this was also the very last time I got drunk but not the last time I drunk alcohol, though I rarely bother.)

I don't remember much about the evening but do remember the officers were invited to the party and encouraged to socialise by dancing with the men. I don't know if the officers chose who they were going to dance with or if it was a random system. I do remember I either managed to find Carol for a dance, or she found me, or it was a random occurrence. Perhaps I secretly found Carol attractive or that dancing with any woman when I was drunk was an opportunity for me. I certainly don't remember dancing with anyone else.

So, there we were face to face with the next song about to start. I clearly remember announcing to Carol that this dance was a 'close dance'. By that I meant a smooch or a slow dance and it had no bearing whatsoever on whatever the song was. I wrapped my arms around her and pressed her body tightly against mine. However, all I can remember of this experience was that I seemed to spend a lot of time treading on her toes. As soon as the dance was finished, she was gone, relieved most likely, and I guess in the circumstances having more than fulfilled her duty. Sorry I was such a drunken oaf Carol.

Black Swans

Plumpton Place is a Jacobean moated manor house owned at the time this story took place, by the billionaire Tom Perkins (since deceased). Dad was his head gardener and since I was in the air force I only went there at weekends, or when I was on leave. There was a large number of ducks that lived in the lakes by the manor house, some wild and some like the Eider ducks purchased by Tom Perkins. There were also a couple of black swans.

The black swans liked to be fed but once you'd fed them would turn on you and try and attack. More than once I'd had to run away from them. They were also very territorial and wherever you went, they went, which could be a bit annoying. However, if you stayed far enough from the edge of the lakes they'd generally stay on the lakes.

One day, or it may have been an evening, I was out with Dad either to feed the ducks, shut the chickens away for the night or maybe just out for a walk. Dad had one of his thumb-sticks with him which he'd made himself. The thumb-stick was about the length, but slightly less thick, than a typical walking stick. We hadn't gone very far before the black swans came to follow us. At one point one of the swans got quite close. Dad turned around and raised the thumb-stick to horizontal level and made a rotating movement with it. All of a sudden, the swan retreated. I think, but I'm not sure, if Dad didn't have to repeat this movement once or even twice more. In any event I was impressed because it seemed like a magic trick to me. I asked him how he did it. He simply replied words to the effect that the swans knew the meaning of the stick.

I was intrigued and asked what 'the meaning of the stick' was, and how had he trained the swans. He laughed and replied that not so long ago he'd got fed up with them trying to attack him and after one did attack him, he brought the thumb-stick down hard across the swan's beak!

Loud Music

At Plumpton, aside from Dad as Head Gardner there was an Estate Manager. I didn't know it till later, but apparently, they weren't both supposed to be off the estate at the same time, something to do with if the burglar alarm went off in the manor house, I guess.

One day I was at Plumpton and Mum and Dad decided to go out for the afternoon. I gave them a few minutes to get clear of the house and then turned on the stereo. The stereo wasn't anything special but the track of the moment was – The Simple Minds 'Up on the catwalk'. It's still one of my favourite tracks. I can't remember if it was the only track I played, or if I played it more than once. However, I do remember that the volume was at max and it was great.

Then, all of a sudden, I saw a fireman run past the lounge window! I jumped up from my seat and turned the volume down or the stereo off, I can't remember which. I was immediately aware of several noises 'Up on the catwalk' had been cloaking: the noise of a fire engine, people running and shouting, and somebody hammering on the back door of our house. I opened the door and it was a fireman. A second fire engine was arriving to join the first fire engine and the fireman asked me if I had a key to the door of the manor house. I replied that I had and I frantically began looking for it.

I found the key and went outside. There was a fire chief's car as well as the two fire engines and one fireman went ahead to tell the fireman considering chopping open the door to the moated manor house that it wouldn't be necessary. I noticed the door also had some wrought iron work on the outside, maybe an outer door or something so I thought that it wouldn't have been easy for them to have broken down.

With the door opened the fire chief asked me if I knew where the fire panel was but I didn't. I told the fireman that we'd have set off the burglar alarm (I knew it was on a direct line to the police) and did he want me to call the police and tell them what was happening or could they do that. He told me he'd do that. A couple of firemen entered the house followed by the fire chief and some sort of senior fireman. I knew that inside the house there was at last one painting worth more than a million pounds along with loads of other valuable stuff. The fire chief became concerned and I heard him tell the senior firemen to 'keep an eye on the lads' or words to that effect!

After a while the fireman assured me that there was no fire and that probably some soot had fallen down the chimney and triggered a smoke detector head. After the fire brigade had left and Dad was back, I told him what had happened though I can't remember if I told him the part about 'Up on the catwalk'. He explained that it was the estate manager's turn to remain at the estate but took me over to the house and showed me where the fire alarm panel was along with the burglar alarm (first door on the left once you were through the main door) in case something similar happened again.

Plumpton Place – the wrong turning

One of Dad's jobs at Plumpton was locking up the house at night and for some reason I can't recall, every room had to be checked. There were a lot of rooms at Plumpton and on one occasion I went with Dad for 'locking up'. We went from room to room and down various corridors and stairs with Dad giving me a commentary as we went. Sometimes there was a room off a room and what Dad described to me as walk-in wardrobe rooms. Then it happened, we were at a dead end when we weren't where we were supposed to be. Dad explained that he must have taken a wrong turn so we doubled back and then carried on until we had finished the job and were back in our own substantially smaller house, Gardeners Cottage.

Plumpton Place – the end

There was not a happy ending for the Stapleton family at Plumpton Place because following the 'hurricane' of October 1987 Dad, just aged forty-nine years old, was killed clearing up the damage of fallen trees. Mum was the same age as my Dad. My sister was twenty-six years old, I was twenty-four years old and my younger brother eighteen years old.

A man in the house

My sister had recently moved to Peterborough and was living in a flat, or a bed sit, and for reasons I can't recall I was visiting her. After drinking at least one mug of tea I needed to use the toilet for a wee. And, while admittedly I didn't normally bother, on this occasion I thought it was best to raise the seat.

As I raised the seat, which was a plain black seat, it was immediately apparent that there was some writing, in what looked to be white typist's correction fluid on the underside of the seat. The writing said 'Yippee, a man in the house'. I never bothered to ask my sister whether she had written the message or whether or was there before she moved in, rather I assumed, rightly or wrongly, that it was her own handiwork.

Car trouble

Mostly on the grounds that I'd incriminate myself, there aren't many motoring stories in this book. However, every now and again I recall one that might be worth a read so it gets added, such as this one.

Just before I was twenty-one years old in 1984, I purchased my car which was almost as old as I was, having been made in 1969. However, not all the experiences were great and from time to time, the car had a problem. In the very early ninetiess after converting the car to very high wattage (but legal) quartz halogen headlamps, I had problems with the electrical charging circuit. While at that time I wasn't a motoring writer (magazine features and books followed some years later) I discovered I knew a Christian writer. In fact, I found out she was an author sometime after we met. She had a boyfriend called Jeremy. Sadly, for her at the time I guess, but not for me, a time came when her and Jeremy were no longer going out with each other. I suppose I wasn't even close to being patient to wait for my opportunity to go out with her myself, since she was very attractive and her book was an amazing read (Puppet on a Chain by Helena Wilkinson). Eventually she agreed to go on a date with me, probably to shut me up and I was really looking forward to spending some time with her. At that time, I lived just outside Thatcham in Berkshire and she lived in Reading and as it turned out the house she lived at, was at the top of a hill. Given that I knew she lived on top of a hill I guess it must have been the second time I went out with her that my 1969 Sprite developed a problem.

I think it happened very shortly after setting out on the drive over to hers that the electrical charging light came on, which meant no electrical charging was occurring! I knew that simply driving the car wouldn't use much of the stored electrical charge in the battery but that starting it would. Also, because she lived on a hill, I hoped I could simply let the car roll down the hill and then bump start the car. I didn't have a backup plan for the bump starting not working, mobile phones hadn't been invented (as far as I know) and I didn't have any kind of breakdown cover. There was also no way I wasn't going to see her. So, with the red warning light glowing on the car's dashboard I duly arrived at hers and we had a lovely time together (I think we went for a walk together unless that was our previous date). When it was time to say goodbye, despite being a summer evening it was also getting dark. I probably told her about the problem with the car, but sure enough it rolled down the hill and bump started ok as I'd hoped.

So far so good I thought, until it began to get dark on the drive home. I suppose I'd wanted to spend as long with Helena as possible and hadn't given the drive home much thought. I'd previous experience of a failed alternator at night on my Mk3 Ford Cortina and that drive home resulted in increasingly slower speeds as the battery discharged due to the current drain of the headlights and that was a shorter drive than this one was going to be. The best solution, it seemed to me, was to drive as close as possible to any car in front of me, which I did, though I can't remember if I even risked putting the sidelights on. This worked well until the car turned off in a different direction to mine, which caused me, at least once from memory, to speed up to catch up another car to follow. Finally, I had to turn off the main road myself and was faced with a drive down some country lanes. With no prospect of being able to follow anyone I would need the headlights on. I figured that the shortest time the headlights were on, the greater my chances of getting back before the battery was totally discharged and left me stranded, and this would be achieved by driving quickly. Needless to say, I made it back ok without drama or incident and felt vindicated in my decision to make the journey and see Helena.

And, the story has a happy ending, because we are still together, the car and myself that is, and we've been having adventures ever since. Helena though, decided I wasn't the right person for her and after the RAF posted me from Berkshire to Suffolk, we lost contact. However, I have never forgotten her grace and kindness to me in the short times we spent together. As for the problems with the car, they were eventually solved by converting it from a dynamo charging system to an alternator charging system.

The RAF Land Rover

At my last RAF posting I was the administrator on a fighter squadron and one of my jobs was to collect the post daily. Since the squadron was the opposite side of the runway to the post room and the rest of the station, I used to use whatever vehicle was available to make the journey there and back. Usually it was an Austin Metro but occasionally it was a Land Rover.

If the vehicle was a Land Rover more often than not, I'd be asked to refuel it. One day, the Land Rover I was using was particularly rubbish and when I parked to refuel it, I discovered the handbrake seemed not to work even when pulled fully up. A Land Rover handbrake isn't on the back wheels like a car, or pretty much any other vehicle, but on the end of the gearbox with the prop-shaft exiting it. On this Land Rover, it was possible to see the handbrake drum and some of the engine's exhaust pipe when the access cover for the fuel tank was lifted. At the refuelling pumps, I lifted the access cover, unfastened the fuel cap and proceeded to fill the tank with red diesel. I'm not sure if it's a feature of all diesels, or just red, but it foamed a lot as I filled the tank resulting in a small amount getting splashed about, including a bit on the exhaust which I guessed wouldn't cause much of a problem.

With the job done, everything back in place and the paperwork signed, I commenced the drive back to the squadron. After a while I noticed a few wisps of smoke emerging from underneath the access cover and I guessed it was the splashed fuel burning off on the exhaust and nothing to worry about. Seconds later the smoke was increasing so I opened the driver's window slightly. The smoke increased in intensity, so I opened the window fully. Then smoke was rapidly filling the cabin and I suddenly realised the handbrake was not only still on, but did work after all! I quickly released it and pulled off the road to let the smoke clear which it gradually did. I then drove slowly back to the squadron and parked the Land Rover. A small amount of smoke was still coming from what I know knew to be the handbrake linings, so rather than hand the keys in and officially return the vehicle, and risk getting into trouble I kept them. Then every quarter of an hour or so I checked to see if the smoke had stopped. When the smoke had finally stopped I simply and discretely returned the keys and nobody was ever any the wiser.

All tickets please

I was travelling back from press day of the London Motor show in 1991, my first on a press pass, with my entourage of two assistants: my brother Phil and a friend Matt. We'd had a great day and we were in high spirits. I even managed to get us in the background while the BBC Motoring programme 'Top Gear' was being filmed and recently even found that episode on 'YouTube'. I was living in Stowmarket at this time and the train was Inter-City rolling stock with a motion detector operated door such that when anyone approached it, it opened with a slightly audible swish, just enough to be noticeable.

It's a ninety-minute journey, and at one point as the sliding door opened, my brother cupped his hands together to slightly muffle his voice and then very loudly said 'All tickets please'. A number of passengers searched and got ready for the non-existent ticket collector, while we laughed as discreetly as we could.

As the journey went on my brother kept repeating the announcement every time someone passed through the door. Since he was sitting facing the door while I was looking down the carriage, he couldn't see the results of all his announcements. On one occasion he asked me 'did anyone look that time' and I had to laugh and reply that some people were still looking for the ticket collector from his previous announcement. As for the real ticket collector – we never saw him or her the whole journey!

Military pyrotechnics

Another name for military pyrotechnics might be 'really big bangers' and in this instance the actual product name is 'Thunder flash'. I'd seen Thunder flashes used on military exercises where the effect is a white flash and a really loud explosion. In the air force, at least, it seems that thunder flashes and other military pyrotechnics don't get used that often and once they have passed, or come close to exceeding their 'use by' date, they have to be disposed of. Of course, they don't get disposed of in the bin or to just anyone, but to a tradesman in the 'armourer' trade.

While I was no longer in the air force, I was living in a rented house shared with one person 'Matt' (an armourer by trade) and another person who was a civilian working for the air force. It was Autumn and not far from the 5th of November when Matt came home from work and announced he had a Thunder flash and suggested he let it off in the (small) back garden of our rented house. I suggested this might not be a good idea as the blast might well shatter one or more of the house windows, and Matt agreed this might be the case. So, we decided to go for a 'drive into the countryside' to let off the thunder flash. We soon found a suitable place to stop – some sort of large concrete hard standing near the entrance to a farmer's field and Matt switched off the car's engine and produced the said item! It became apparent, and I checked this was the case, as Matt read the instructions that he had never used a thunder flash before. Still what could go wrong except for Matt to announce it was lit, while we were still in the car. I shouted for him to throw it away, which he did – underneath his car. Matt then scrambled for the keys in the ignition to start his car and drive away. As I looked back into the pitch black of the country side there was an enormous red coloured explosion followed almost instantly by a large bang which he laughed at in amusement. After that we stuck to 'regular' fireworks.

A new Stereo

Actually, this story isn't about a new stereo but a second-hand one, what might be politely called pre-owned today. The original owner was my brother and the owner before myself was my sister and I'm not sure if it hadn't also been my Mum's at one point. It was a Denon amplifier with a twin cassette desk and a radio, also known as Hi-fi separates. Even second-hand it was considerably better than most, if not all Sony or Technics products at that time. It also come with a pair of suitably large Mission 707 speakers.

With everything delivered and set-up it was soon apparent that not only was the sound quality considerably better than my old Amstrad it was also capable of much greater volume. In fact, the volume potential was so great I had to wait for a suitable opportunity to test it, nothing new there then!

At this time, I shared a rented semi-detached house with two colleagues from the RAF (though I'd since left enlisted service). I had to wait for the neighbour of the other half of the semi to go out with his wife (not sure if they had a baby by this time or not) while the house on the other side of the house was empty and unoccupied (possibly a mortgagee repossession). It was a warm summer day and I had the bedroom windows open with the stereo in my bedroom. I only played a couple of tracks at full volume, though it may have been more. One track was 'Satisfaction' by the Rolling Stones. Certainly, it didn't take long for my ears to ring. With the test complete and the volume turned down I was aware that someone was ringing the doorbell of the house. Noise complaint I thought as I went downstairs to answer the door. Living in a small Close I was fairly familiar with what all the neighbours looked like, even though I didn't know their names, but I had given them nicknames.

I answered the door and a man who I didn't recognise as one my neighbours, who looked incredibly sheepish, asked with a degree of embarrassment if I could turn my music down. I replied that of course I would, and of course I already had. Once he had left, I raced upstairs to look out of the window to see where he had come from. I saw him walk out of the Close and around the corner before disappearing out of sight. Bloody good stereo that, I thought.

But, that's not the end of the story. Later that day when the neighbour returned I either bumped into him or he dropped by for a chat. He mentioned that he'd heard I was playing the Rolling Stones earlier and I asked how he knew that. He explained that his Uncle was staying at his for a few days and that while he'd gone out his Uncle had stayed in and heard my music (which was hardly surprising). He then laughed and explained that some bloke had knocked on his door and when his Uncle had answered it was subject to an aggressive complaint using a lot of words that began with the letter F about loud music. His Uncle had replied in a similar manner finishing with the fact that it wasn't his music but the person next door. The mystery was thus solved about the sheepish look and very polite complaint.

Bread and Wine in Sardinia

Being in the RAF and a committed Christian (I made my commitment on Good Friday, 1988) often resulted in my attending a church other than my local one whether because I was on a training course or on 'detachment' outside the United Kingdom. The other thing about being in the RAF and a committed Christian was that wherever you went you soon met other members of the 'God Squad'.

Having arrived in Sardinia on detachment with members of my home 'squad' it wasn't long before I met one of the Sardinian 'squad' and he told us about an English-speaking church we could go to on Sunday. As it turned out, this English-speaking church was some kind of American protestant denomination nearer the formal or high church end of the range of the spectrum and not quite what I was either used to, or preferred. Still, I'd been to a fairly diverse range of churches including: Baptist, Pentecostal, Evangelical and lots of different Church of England churches. The message was pretty much the same but traditions and customs varied, including the bread and wine.

What I call bread and wine some churches call something else, some grander, some less so, and some I consider pretentious. The basis of all however, was that food, be it actual bread torn from a roll or loaf of bread, a neatly cut square of bread from a sliced loaf, an embossed rice paper type wafer, or a piece of a large wafer, was served to each person one at a time. It might be delivered at your seat or at the altar and you might be sitting, standing or kneeling. Next would come liquid which might be wine or Ribena or some other sweet red fruit juice either served in a chalice (a silver goblet) passed from person to person and wiped in-between, or in a pewter or glass or plastic miniature container about the size of a large sewing thimble, per person.

I figured I pretty much had seen all the variations possible, so being in an unfamiliar church didn't give me any anxiety. Still when we came to that part of the service when we'd receive bread and wine, I was slightly surprised that everyone got up from their seat and had to form a really large circle. Then the church minister went from person to person with the bread, only it looked like a large poppadum and each person had a piece broken off from it. I've never been one for doing what everyone else does for the sake of it, and so even in a church sense I'm not much of a 'sheep'. So, while I saw everyone still holding their bread/poppadum for what seemed to me to be no good reason, I did what I'd always done and ate mine straight off. Next the wine was being administered and I immediately saw that while there were 2 chalices no-one drank from them. What happened was that they dipped the bread into one or the other and then ate it. I'd obviously eaten my bread and experienced the feeling of 'creeping death' as the church minister gradually got nearer to me.

The obvious course of action was to do nothing and simply let the wine pass by, but for reasons I won't go into, I wasn't going to do that. The 'squad' member next to me wasn't going to divide his piece of bread into a smaller piece and in fact he might even have been sniggering unkindly at my predicament. The other obvious course of action was to simply sip from the cup being pretty much the Church of England tradition. So, the minister reached me and stopped. I pulled a facial expression nodding down to the chalice so he'd understand what I needed to do. His responding facial expression was quizzical and so without further ado I quickly grasped the chalice, took a sip and passed it back to him. His facial expression was one of shock and horror at what I'd done, which I hardly thought was sacrilegious, and before I'd even had time to think about it, he had moved onto the next person. I laughed about it afterwards and though the shock of my actions served him right for not explaining, for the benefit of visitors, how things worked in his church, which is after all what all good churches do in my wide experience as a visitor.

Guns for hire

As an enlisted serviceman in the RAF I got to fire a gun, usually once a year. 'Course it wasn't called a gun but rather by its correct title, being either a rifle, a sub-machine gun (smg/smig) or a pistol. There were other times when I didn't fire a gun but I'd be issued one and neither of the two most likely reasons held much appeal to me: a ceremonial parade, or a military exercise.

At RAF Wattisham a military exercise, for myself, mean being locked in a concrete bunker for two or three days. One of my few tasks was to issue pistols to anyone who had a reason for having one. I had three boxes of them. One small box held 9mm Browning's for Engineering Officers, while the other boxes held the smaller calibre 7.62 mm Walther's for aircrew. Each pistol had its own specific type of shoulder holster. The Browning, which was by far the larger pistol, had a leather holster, while the Walther had a small holster with multiple straps which some of the aircrew dubbed 'the bra'.
For the most part on exercise, in the bunker, meant hanging around and not doing much in particular and sometimes I got bored. The squadron had a mixture of characters, some of which were ok and some who weren't.

On one particular exercise, I got very bored. To break the monotony, I had a look at the shoulder holster for the Browning pistol and realised that it was large enough to fit around my waist, like a cowboy holster, so I fastened it accordingly. Then for good measure I put one on the other side to make an albeit mis-matched, pair. I put a Browning in each and then with my hands on the pistol butts I walked slowly to the main part of the bunker with my best imitation of a western cowboy's sneer.

I received a mixed response but the two I remember were contrasting. One Chief Technician looked cross and was about to let me know how much trouble I was in. But, before he had chance to say anything, the Junior Engineering Officer (he was ok and drove an MG Midget) laughed and exclaimed 'you look very punchy Corporal Stapleton'! With my impersonation 'delivered' I returned to my part of the bunker and put the pistols and holsters back and wondered how much longer the boredom would last.

Supersonic flight

During my time in the RAF I'd taken every opportunity I could to fly in a plane, and had flights that including parachutist drops, and air to air refuelling, all from the back of a Hercules C130 aircraft. At the end of my service in the RAF and my time on 74 'Tiger' Sqn I was treated to the pinnacle of my flying experience – a supersonic flight in a Phantom F4J. I forgot when I was told I was getting the trip but because an F4J is a 'fast jet' with an ejection seat it was necessary to undergo close to a half day's briefing on all the necessary safety drills. I was told exactly what would happen if I had to eject, from the moment I pulled the ejection handle, to when I landed via parachute on the ground. After a while I wasn't sure whether or not some procedures had to be executed manually or if they were meant to happen automatically but if the automatic procedure failed, I'd need to operate things manually, like seat separation. In the end, I just nodded periodically and thought if I had to eject, I'd just pull the handle and hope for the best!

Because my flight was in a fighter aircraft that can, and would, 'pull' high levels of gravity force - 'g force', it was necessary to wear what is called a 'g suit' or 'g pants' which are over trousers that prevent all the blood rushing from your head to your feet and thus causing you to blackout when high, and sustained high, 'g' forces are 'pulled' by the aircraft. Also, because it was Autumn going into Winter, I had to wear an immersion suit which is very similar to a diving dry suit, the differences being it is adapted for a connection for the 'g suit'. So, if the aircraft had to ditch in the sea (the North Sea for my trip) I would not immediately die from exposure or hypothermia but would live long enough to be rescued.

Both the 'g suit' and immersion suit had to be fitted by the Sqn's survival equipment fitters and to this day I'm not certain if some of their advice was a set up to try and make me air sick. I was advised it was 'very cold up there' which seemed reasonable enough to me having flown in unpressurised aircraft but not considering the F4J was a pressurised aircraft. It was suggested to me, and I agreed that I'd need to wear thermal underwear and the RAF wool jumper under the flying suit and probably the jumper was a garment in excess of what was required. Still once kitted out, including with a helmet, it was time for the trip and somewhat awkwardly I walked to the jet and climbed in.

The ground crew strapped me into the seat, connected: the 'g suit', oxygen supply, and radio lead, also doing likewise to the pilot and it was time to go. At this point the first snag occurred because the pilot (talking to me over the radio) asked me to close my canopy and I hadn't been told how to during the briefing. It didn't take long though for the pilot to explain which lever to operate and my canopy was shut and with his already shut, we were taxiing for take-off. The pilot was very helpful and friendly, putting me fully at ease, though I was in fact fairly relaxed, and explained about something called V1 and V2 or something like that. These are the points at which take off may be abandoned if something is going wrong or if take off has to occur even if something is going wrong. I acknowledged his information and the aircraft was lined up for take-off.

As we took off it was apparent to me that both the take-off speed and angle of climb once we'd left the runway, were dramatic compared to taking off in a civil airliner. We soon cleared the clouds and were cruising sub-sonic in glorious sunshine with the cloud below us. At this point the second snag occurred. The pilot wanted a radar picture and asked me to get him one! I was already slightly warmer than I'd liked and leaning forward and with my head down fiddling with some knobs on the radar wasn't what I wanted to be doing. Nonetheless I managed to get him a satisfactory picture (I assume he had a screen in the front that was linked to mine in the back). I relaxed and not long after I did so I heard over my helmet radio some air traffic information. Most of it made no sense to me apart from one word 'traffic' which I knew meant another plane. Then it happened!

In a blink of an eye the aircraft had banked at least 90 degrees and turned at probably a similar amount, I can't be sure because it happened quicker than I'd believed possible and certainly with more drama than any plane I'd been in before including some pretty tight turns I'd made as glider pilot (and got in trouble for). I remembered that if you felt sick flying it was supposed to help if you breathed 100% pure oxygen and I lifted my hand to my oxygen mask and flicked the lever from air/oxygen mix to 100% pure and gulped hard several times. Oxygen is supposed to have no taste but to my palate at that time, and throughout the flight, it tasted sweet to me. The drama was over as quick as it had begun and we were soon back on a straight and level flight. I looked out of the cockpit and there a long way, or so it seemed to me below us, was an American KC135 tanker aircraft that passed from our left to right and then was gone. The pilot apologised for the sudden manoeuvre and asked if I was ok. I said I was ok and in what turned out to be a 'self-fulfilling prophecy' replied that I'd probably be sick in about ten minutes.

One thing I knew about being sick in a fast jet is that if any sick went into the oxygen mask, which also contained the radio microphone, it would be the job of the person making the mess to clear it up. So, I switched off the microphone so the pilot wouldn't be deafened by my retching and unclipped the mask from my face and neatly made the first deposit into the bag, NATO air sickness, provided for that purpose.

We flew out across The Wash, and the pilot told me he was going to fly the plane at a supersonic speed. As we accelerated it was hard to see the increase in speed without much of a reference but there was a small amount of buffeting as we went through the sound barrier each time. That's correct, twice the speed of sound, and although the Phantom was an old aircraft even in 1990 when I made my flight, at the time it was built in the late 1950s it held world speed records with a maximum speed of Mach 2.2.

After flying supersonic we climbed and then headed north ready for a low-level flight entering a pre-booked low flying area near Bridlington. The descent into the low flying area was unpleasant since it was like being a lift or elevator for several minutes, maybe even more than 5 minutes, and I was sick again a couple of times.

The low flying was exhilarating and since I'd not long been sick, I felt well enough to enjoy it since while being fast it was low enough to see sheep running around in the fields and I even saw Cadwell Park racing circuit. While the trip was uneventful it was the case that back on the squadron at least one noise complaint was received for our trip which I could hear the pilot dealing with in the next office to mine back on the Sqn headquarters after we'd returned. One souvenir I have from my flight is a colour photocopy of the map used to plot the low-level trip which is now proudly framed and displayed on a wall here at my home.

Back in the Phantom, the pilot asked me if I wanted to carry on do the 'south coast tour' and some aerobatics, or if I wanted to return back to the squadron. Well as I type this, I wish I had done the full tour but at the time, I'd been pretty sick and felt pretty awful so while not having to have an early return after thirty minutes, as had been the case with some of my colleagues, managing in all about an hour, it was long enough for me. We were close to Wattisham and getting ready to land when I could hear what seemed to me some amazingly appalling air traffic communication. Unless I'm mistaken one controller even had what sounded like an edge of panic in his voice at one point. It was clear we were placed in some kind of holding pattern and the pilot was unimpressed stating 'we have to put up with this (rubbish?) every day' or words to that effect. He told me we didn't have to wait and that since I wasn't well, we could land quicker. I advised him I was ok and as it turned out had finished being sick for the last time a few minutes earlier. However, he made a radio call that included the words 'sick P.O.B' which I later realised meant sick passenger on board with myself being the passenger, and very promptly after that call, we landed.

A funny thing happened then, because as we taxied to the squadron an ambulance followed us in to the hardened aircraft shelter (HAS). I opened the canopy and a medic looked up at me and asked I was ok. I explained that I'd been sick but that I was now ok. He double checked I was ok and then left.

The ground crew technician that came to unstrap me was Pete James and he didn't seem that pleased to see me. This wasn't because that while we hadn't always got on, we'd got over that, but probably because I was admin rather than engineering, and he hadn't yet had a trip in a Phantom. I gave him a smile and held up the very full back of sick and it diffused the moment and he laughed.

Before long I was back at my desk as if nothing had ever happened, I felt good, and apart from an occasional enquiry I had to field about what the ambulance's appearance was for, the day finished without further comment.

A training course

Having left the air force and started a new job I had to go on an introductory training course which was a two-week residential course at a nice hotel in Sudbury, Suffolk. It was quite different and much less formal than any training course in the air force and the layout for the room was what I subsequently learned was called 'horseshoe' but which at the time I'd call a semi-circle.

It so happened that the woman who sat opposite me, and we sat in the same seats every day, wore stockings and suspenders. While relatively young and definitely single and as red-blooded as the next man, she was probably older than myself and not really my type and so I wasn't 'interested'. Still every day, by accident or design, she revealed her thighs complete with stockings and suspenders and I became accustomed to looking and seeing this and eventually never gave it a second thought.

One day I came to the course room but found some old guy had taken my seat. Apparently, this old guy was the trainers' manager and was going to sit in on the course all day and I thought nothing more of it. I guess I found another seat or a seat was found for me and the day proceeded much as usual. However, at break time I found one of the trainers berating the woman who I'd usually sat opposite and the trainer seeing me, turned to me in a flash. She began 'and as for you, why didn't you say she was wearing stockings and suspenders, we (meaning herself and the other trainer) thought the silly old sod was going to have a heart attack!' Well there wasn't much I could say politely was there and while I can't remember for certain, I think there was a change in seating after the break.

An encounter with the RSPCA

While living in Stowmarket I was on my way home one evening via the supermarket and by chance happened to see a cat just about to pounce on a bird in the local church's graveyard/the greensward. I shooed the cat away and wasn't sure if the cat had already attacked the bird or not but decided its best chance was for me to rescue it. So, I gently scooped it into my rucksack. Once home one of the guys who I shared the house with produced a cardboard shoe box and the bird was transferred into it.

It seemed the best thing to do, to help the bird, was for me to ring the Royal Society for the Prevention of Cruelty to Animals (RSPCA), so I did. The RSPCA either advised me they'd send an inspector round or maybe they just said they'd send someone round. In either case my expectation was that a tall man, with slightly greying hair, in blue uniform with a peaked cap and the letters RSPCA on it would turn up to look at the bird. Eventually the doorbell rang and I may or may not have seen an RSPCA vehicle parked outside the house. But since callers were rare, I expected the caller to be the RSPCA. I opened the door and Wow! I guess I must have looked surprised and not just because the RSPCA had sent a woman. But this wasn't just any woman, it was a woman with the most amazing softest brown eyes ever. She wasn't surprised to see me, nor I guess my surprised look – probably she had that effect on every man she met for the first time.

She came into the lounge and asked to have a look at the bird. I explained I wasn't sure if it was still alive and she removed the shoe box lid at ground level. As soon as she did this the bird jumped out of the box and ran across my foot doing a little white birdie poo on it as it did so. She announced, with a smile that the bird certainly seemed to be alive now and almost immediately caught it with her hands which impressed me. Then and now, I'm not really an animal person but at that time I was thinking that maybe I could become an animal person.

Brown eyes advised me: the bird was a fledgling, the cat would have got it, and that I should release it in a safe place near to where I found it. So, the bird lived another day at least and while I think I rang the RSPCA to tell them I'd done as directed, I've never had another encounter with the RSPCA since.

The wrong kind of snow

Having left the air force while living in a rented house in Stowmarket, Suffolk I'd started commuting to a job in London. It wasn't really planned that way but I had no alternative. The commute was five minutes' walk to the train station, ninety minutes on the train, twenty minutes on the tube and five minutes walking. It all added up to a two hour commute each way if the train was on time and often it wasn't. The delay could easily be over an hour.

One day, having arrived at work at my usual time of about 0830, a couple of hours later it began to snow. It wasn't snowing heavily but from about 1030 onwards I noticed people leaving the office to go home which struck me as a bit odd. The internet didn't exist at this time and if you wanted weather news, I supposed you had to have a radio and I didn't. My manager's manager suggested I ought to think about going home, which surprised me and I said I'd be ok. He repeated this suggestion at least twice more over the next hour and in the end, I thought if the silly sod wants me to go home early I might as well. It wasn't long though before I realised that it was looking like I was the silly sod, not him!

At the underground station I found not many trains were running and rather than wait a couple of minutes for a train, it was going to be more like half an hour. Later in my commuting experience I found I could walk in less time than the underground took, taking a direct route, and save myself some money as well.

The sight at Liverpool Street station wasn't encouraging either. No trains had left for Suffolk for some time and apparently none might leave at all that day. It had never occurred to me that I might be stranded in London and I'm not sure if I even had any telephone numbers with me for anyone that lived inside the M25. The concourse was packed and par for the course for this type of fiasco, there was scant or no information on what was or wasn't happening. I worked out the most likely train and platform leaving for Suffolk and managed to squeeze onto it. I'd hoped to get into the toilet but learned there were already five, yes five people already crammed in it. So, I was stuck in the vestibule area for the departure out of the station. I subsequently learnt people were fighting on the platform to get onto the train and even people hanging off it as it departed.

About five or ten minutes into the journey the locomotive broke down, at London Stratford. After what was close to an hour standing, squashed so I couldn't move, the train began to move again. However, while this train was an 'express' service scheduled to stop three times before my stop, with a journey time of ninety minutes it was stopping at every single station on the route and not travelling very fast at all. I wasn't particularly aware of what the time was but I guess after more than another hour I eventually got to stand someone less packed and then some time after that I got a seat. I remember one time looking out of the window when the train had stopped in the middle of nowhere that it was blowing a blizzard outside. Another time it stopped I could see what looked to be trackside workers who were perhaps working on the points. There were no longer many people on the train when I might still have expected it to be fairly full. I wondered if the train would get stranded in the middle of no-where and I might end up having to spend the night on the train.

Eventually the train pulled into Stowmarket, at a quarter to nine in the evening. I was safely home on what I learned afterwards was the last train that left London for Suffolk for more than two days.

Singing in the Philippines

As a kid at primary school every year, along with all the other kids I was forced to audition for the school choir for the school Christmas concert. I always hated this because I knew I had a rotten singing voice and after the first year I also knew I'd end in the group that did something called 'Choral Speaking'. Nonetheless, year after year, I was forced and humiliated by having to prove that I didn't have a good or even average singing voice.

Fast forward some decades later and not only having become a born-again or committed Christian I found myself on a part evangelical, part relief 'mission' (though not quite in the sense of the 'Blue's brothers' on a mission from God) in the Philippines. While a few years of singing in church had improved my singing slightly, I was still no choirboy (or adult chorister).

Towards the end of our time on the mission, at our host church, for some reason, we were all invited to go to the front of the church on a raised platform/stage and sing together. I was reluctant to do so but obliged. Then once on the platform/stage I was given a microphone. While I can't sing, I do know how to switch off a microphone and so promptly, but discreetly switched, mine off.

Soon the time came to sing and I noticed that a young woman was in charge of the sound mixing desk and was looking to and fro at us while adjusting the desk controls. Unfortunately, it wasn't long before she kept looking at me, then at the controls and then back at me. She may have even checked the microphone lead at her end. I felt sorry for her because there she was trying to do her best, for me, a guest from the other side of the world, not knowing I have an awful singing voice. I also felt bad that I'd switched off the microphone but balanced that with my having been placed in a difficult position obligated to something I simply lacked the skills to do. I was relieved when the song ended, smiled politely and can't recall whether I switched the microphone back on or not. Still, I'd at least saved the church congregation from an awful noise that would have been my amplified singing voice.

Honeymoon Oops

After getting married in Northampton, my wife and I took our honeymoon in Cyprus, staying in a small house in a village halfway up the Troodos mountains. As part of the holiday we had a hire car which was a fairly clapped-out Mk3 Escort that had a rattily engine that sounded like a diesel. It was fairly gutless as well, being I guess, a basic 1.3L and it was slow driving up the mountain to our holiday home, the first day and every other day.

I'd been to Cyprus before, but my wife hadn't, and so I had a reasonable idea of those things I wanted to take her to see and those things I'd never seen before that I thought we could visit together. Fairly early on in our honeymoon I suggested, and it was agreed, we would go to Paphos for the day. The main road route was all the way down the mountain to meet the coast road and then all the way along the coast road. Not only did that look as if it would take longer than finding a more direct route, we were on a tight budget for money, so if we could save money on petrol we would. It was of course possible to coast down the road to the, well, coast road, with the engine switched off. However, looking at our basic map of Cyprus I was confident of being able to navigate cross country to Pathos.

At this point in the story it's safe for me to say that if you are a man you may find the story funny but if you are a woman you might not.

I don't recall discovering my wife didn't like map reading and we did have a bit off difficulty with the navigation, not least because some roads seemed to be poorly marked, or not marked at all. Cyprus hosts a car rally, which at that time I think was a full international event, and was not due to happen until after we would be safely back in the UK. Still, there was a chance I might drive over the very same rough roads the rally would go on. Those rough roads inexplicably would cease to be black tarmac and become crushed or rolled rock/stone. It was also the case that as quickly as they stopped being black tarmac, they might become black tarmac again. Often the roads wound round and up a steep incline or down a steep descent. Consequently, the view from one side of the car would be the hillside and on the other, usually the driver's side, a steep drop. I found this drive to be both quite an exhilarating cross-country drive and fun, and drove accordingly, though generally in second or third gear and with a measure of caution, in my opinion and experience. My wife wasn't sharing my enjoyment of the drive and was concerned at the sheer drops she could see from time to time. I nodded to her concerns while explaining it was just like the rally of Cyprus as our passage raised a cloud of dust and the engine revved away.

Suddenly I was aware that my wife, of a few days, had ceased to voice her concerns and when I looked across at her I could see that she was sobbing with fear and tears ran down her cheeks. So, oops, there it was, I'd only been married a few days and I'd manage to frighten my wife with my driving, and made her cry. I slowed down after that and we reached Pathos safely. 'Course we took the main roads back to our holiday let in the village.

Manchester proposition

At one time my work used to take me quite regularly to Manchester which involved a reasonably pleasant train journey. Sometimes I even got to travel first class. I preferred to walk from the train station (Manchester Piccadilly) to the office and likewise back. I never realised at the time that this walk took me through once of the less desirable parts of the city.

One day as I was walking back to the station, I noticed a woman ahead of me, possibly on a street corner. As I got nearer, I noticed what I thought to myself was an uncommonly short skirt. Then I thought, 'hang on a minute' and decided that rather than get a really good look, it was better to keep my eyes fixed in front of me and walk straight ahead. I stuck to my plan, though in my peripheral vision it seemed that the woman may well have been wearing some sort of mesh or string vest with little or nothing underneath it.

The woman spoke to me as I approached her and for some reason, I didn't actually hear what she had said but shook my head as a 'no-thanks'. She was obviously either annoyed, disappointed or displeased by this and I did clearly hear her say 'you don't know what you're missing'. To which my thought was 'probably my train'.

The TENS machine

Expectant mothers in the late nineteen nineties had a new and additional option to manage the pain of child birth as an alternative to gas and air, pethidine or epidural anaesthetic. This was TENS (Transcutaneous electrical nerve stimulation) which was administered by a small battery-operated device and some adhesive pads connected by wires to the device. The devices were expensive to buy and so maternity units loaned them to patients against a refundable deposit. The sticky pads were disposed of after use. Isobel have collected it from the maternity unit passed it to me to look at. Since it seemed I'd be the one at the controls for the machine I had it out of the box and was reading the instructions. While reading them I was interrupted by the arrival of my wife's younger brother, who for some reason took an interest in the device. After a short discussion, we agreed I'd give him a small demonstration. So, I peeled the corner back of a pad and he stuck it to his finger. He may even have had another pad on a finger of his other hand. I proceeded to rotate the dial to see if he could feel anything.

'No' he replied, 'nothing' he replied and so I gradually rotated the dial to increasingly higher settings. Perhaps the device was broken or had a flat battery we speculated as the dial finished up near the maximum setting. Then I found the problem was that there was an on/off switch and it was switched off. I threw the switch to 'on' and several things happened at once. Firstly, he threw his hands wildly up into the air and secondly, he shouted in a quavering voice 'YEESSSSSS'. I switched the device off and laughed loudly and while he did see funny side of the test, was prompt in removing the pad or pads. Come the actual moment of birth pangs my wife did use the TENS machine but at some point, chose to abandon it and due to other medical reasons had an epidural anaesthetic.

Saying Goodbye to Grandma

My Grandma on Mum's side grew ill with dementia as she grew older which in some ways was sad and other ways funny. I'd never got on that well with her, when I was a kid, nor her get on with me. However, in her final years we both must have mellowed, albeit in different ways. One year I had a Christmas card that said 'to grandma' and 'from grandma' written in her very spidery writing. Eventually my Uncles decided it would be best and safest for her to spend her final years in an old people's home and arranged for this to happen. They told her that she was going on holiday so as not to upset her. However, as things turned out this move was delayed, as she had a stroke and had to go in hospital and I decided to visit her. We were living in Northampton and Faye was less than 3 months old. It was cold and foggy as we wrapped Faye up and got on a bus to visit her in Peterborough Hospital.

When we arrived at the hospital, I found Grandma in very good cheer, though in a ward with strange characters. One old lady whispered to us that once you came in, they didn't let you out. Clearly Grandma was going no-where as she was in a seat with something like a writing table attached to it that prevented her getting out from it without assistance from someone else. Grandma was pleased to meet Faye and made a fuss of her. From time to time Grandma commented that 'she wouldn't come here again' and 'they don't like after you very well'. It took me a while to realise that having been told she was going on holiday, and knowing that she wasn't in her own home, she believed she was on holiday. The hospital, therefore, was to her a guest house or hotel that didn't live up to her expectations though she was very polite in the way she passed comment. Grandma clearly didn't have plans to stay and wanted to leave. Once she asked us if we could put her on a bus so she could go home. Another time she asked if we'd walk with her to the end of a road and the bus stop. Each time she asked I had to reply and tell her that I was sorry but I wasn't able to do this. I don't think I gave her a reason why and she seemed not to mind though some minutes later she would ask again in a slightly re-phrased way. It was sad that Grandma wasn't where she wanted to be but since she'd had major surgery only a day or so previously, I didn't feel any guilt for not helping her home. However, while she didn't plan on returning it wasn't so bad that she made any specific complaint. All the old ladies in her ward were very pleased to meet Baby Faye and she was carefully passed around to all who wanted to see her. One lady insisted on giving Isobel some 'money for the baby' and pressed something into Isobel's hand. Eventually we had to leave to catch the bus home and said goodbye to Grandma who while clearly pleased to see us may not have realised who we were or that she'd met her first great grand-daughter (she had until then only great grandsons). After we'd left the ward, I asked Isobel how much money the old lady had given Faye and Isobel explained that she not given her anything at all but had perhaps imagined she'd given her some money.

Grandma never did return home because not long after our visit she died peacefully on Christmas day.

Faye – after Christmas

It wasn't that long after Christmas and Faye was not yet old enough to go to school and I was ill in bed at home. I'm not sure where Isobel was but suddenly Faye burst into the bedroom and spoke probably the longest sentence, I'd heard her say up to then. 'I want toys, presents in boxes' she told me. I replied that I was very sorry but I didn't have any. She briefly acknowledged my response and as suddenly as she'd arrived, she'd left. As I pondered this event, I realised that probably the only previous occasion until then that she'd been in our bedroom was Christmas morning not long gone, when all her Christmas presents were in our room waiting for her to unwrap.

Trouble with Gubs

When Faye was a toddler, and still learning to speak, she had a large vocabulary, albeit she had to modify some words to be able to speak them. One such word was 'gloves' which she modified to 'gubs'. She had her gloves, probably mittens and I had my gloves. Mine weren't particularly waterproof and sometimes I used to place them on the lounge radiator to dry out.

Something I learned about being a parent fairly early on, is that children need to be closely supervised at all times. Also, that even if you aren't watching them, then they are either watching you, or they are up to some sort of mischief. So, returning to use my gloves probably directly after Christmas/New Year, after they had been drying as per usual, I found that I couldn't get them on. The problem seemed to be that I couldn't get my fingers down deep enough into the finger sockets. I ceased attempting to put them on and looked to see if I could find out what the problem was. I discovered that a small hazelnut/cobb/filbert nut still in its shell had been rammed down the finger socket of the glove. In fact, every finger socket of each glove had a single nut in it. It took me a while to remove them and since we didn't have a squirrel in the house, I realised that this must have been one of Faye's unsupervised adventures.

The cellar

The first house I purchased (with a mortgage) was a two-bedroom terrace house in Northampton. It also remains the only house I've ever lived in that had a cellar. I really liked the cellar because it also had a bench and a vice and plenty of room to store my tool-kit, spare parts for my car and anything that I didn't mind getting damp. After getting married to Isobel she moved in with me as my wife. Just over a year later Faye was born and she lived and grew up in that house. The cellar had a door from the kitchen and mostly Faye wasn't allowed in the kitchen but did have to pass through it to get to the back door and the garden.

From the outset Faye could be both determined and adventurous and I not only didn't want her to fall down the cellar steps, I didn't want her going down there and exploring my stuff. I think there was a small bolt at the top of the door that she couldn't see let alone reach. However, I might occasionally forget to secure the bolt or I guessed that even with the brute force a four and eventually five-year-old child could muster, it would yield.

So, to discourage Faye from even thinking about going down the cellar I told her that was where a monster lived. Since actions speak louder than words, I backed up the monster story with a bit of an act whenever I came up from the cellar or whenever she was in the kitchen, or passing through it and looked at the cellar door. What I would do is open and shut the door as if something was pulling on the other side of the door handle and shout for the monster to get back before finally shutting it. It also happened that while the cellar steps were dark and so was the cellar itself because you also had to go down by whatever light shown down from the kitchen until you got to the bottom and reached and turned on the cellar light.

Faye was never seemingly wholly convinced there was a monster in the cellar but she was also never wholly convinced there wasn't either, and never went down, not even once. In fact, when her cousins of a similar age visited and stayed with us for a few days I told them the same story and acted out the routine for them, which pretty much had the same effect of creating enough uncertainty for them to not to risk venturing down the steps though the oldest being slightly older than Faye seemed less than convinced.

Screaming at night

Once in Melville Street, Northampton, I was woken up by Faye (no more than age six) screaming in the middle of the night (subsequently found to be about half past one in the morning). I jumped up out of bed and ran across the landing to her bedroom and turned on the light. I asked her what the matter was. She calmly replied 'a bee was on me'. I soon realised that she had of course been dreaming and soon everyone was safely back asleep.

Time to get up

"A twenty to ten, time to get up, a twenty to ten, time to get up" Faye was calling to me, having entered our bedroom, while I was asleep in bed. It was Sunday morning and twenty to ten was the time for me to get up and go to church. Getting me out of bed on a Sunday morning was one of Faye's small jobs as a toddler and one which my wife gave her to do. I felt really tired and went back to sleep. Faye however, wasn't one to give up and after a while returned once more calling "A twenty to ten, time to get up, a twenty to ten, time to get up." I still felt tired and ignored her. She didn't give up though and as I was woken once more, I decided I was just too tired to get up and go to church but couldn't really understand why, and went back to sleep.

What seemed like an hour later Faye returned once more and announced "a twenty to ten, time to get up, a twenty to ten, time to get up." I knew it couldn't still be twenty to ten by now so reached out of my bed to find my alarm clock and establish what the real time was. I don't remember the exact time but it was something like half past eight and Faye must have trying to get me up for over an hour if not longer. I went back to sleep and got up much later and told my wife who laughed, not realising that Faye had been trying to get me up. Faye was too small to be able to tell the time and relied on my wife's prompt on a Sunday morning but I guess on this morning she'd decided she knew how the 'routine' worked and didn't need my wife to tell her what to do (or when) and had simply got on with the job herself of getting me out of bed by telling me 'a twenty to ten, time to get up, a twenty to ten, time to get up'.

First time at crèche

Faye was our first daughter and when she was a small girl, we had never left her with any other parent or babysitter or relative nor nursery school, but realised that one day we surely would. As things turned out the first time, we would leave her with anyone, it would be the crèche at Sunday School. We explained to her that: we'd be leaving her and collecting her later, she'd be safe, they'd be nothing to be worried about and that if she needed us, we'd be in church.

When Sunday arrived, we apprehensively took her to the crèche. We weren't the first to arrive and several children were already in the crèche playing with toys. Faye was very interested in the toys and the children and instead of giving us a kiss goodbye, immediately left us without looking back. She put one hand in the air and said 'bye, bye'. We were both amused and relieved that there had been nothing to worry about and went off to the church service.

After church had finished, we went to collect Faye from the crèche. Unfortunately collecting Faye did not run as smoothly as dropping her off had, as the moment she saw us she started crying. The crying turned into screaming and shouting as she told us to 'go away, go away'. Several of the other parents looked at this scene in surprise and we felt awkward.

Unfortunately, this episode wasn't a one off and in the coming Sundays while we never, ever, had trouble dropping Faye off at crèche, collecting was much the same as that first collection had been, for several weeks. Clearly playing with the toys in crèche was far more appealing than being with us!

Mail order

When Faye was about six years old, I had a mail order catalogue for discontinued motorsports clothing such as t-shirts and sweatshirts, though the catalogue also contained badges and key-rings. At that time, money was always tight and I made a small and prudent selection that I circled in the catalogue with instructions to my wife to order for me, I guess by ringing through using her bank card, for which I'd repay her. A few days later a parcel duly arrived but my good mood soon turned to bad, when I opened it to find a whole pile of badges and key-rings I hadn't ordered but had seemingly paid for. I shouted at my wife 'why did you order all this stuff'? She replied in all innocence 'but you marked them in the catalogue'. Clearly, I hadn't and so the catalogue was produced by myself and I showed her my items circled whereupon she showed me the key-rings and badges ticked. Of course, I hadn't ticked them and while we commenced to blame each other a small voice announced 'it was me'.
We both looked at Faye in speechless surprise and the argument deflated.

I paid my wife for all the extra items and for the next couple of years' birthday parties the party bags had discontinued motorsports badges and key-rings in them, thanks to Faye.

The book

I can't remember where I found it, but find it I did, and 'it' was a ripped book. I was disappointed that Faye had ripped one of her own story books and decided we needed to talk about it. At this time Faye was probably four or five years old. Faye was in her bedroom and it was probably round about bedtime when I got to speak to her. I did my best to put on a serious expression and tone of voice. I showed her the ripped book and asked her 'how did this get ripped'? Faye shrugged her shoulders without a care in the world and simply replied 'it must have ripped by itself'? Clearly that wasn't the case but I was taken aback both by her reply and casual manner so I was momentarily speechless, and can't recall if I challenged her obvious lie. On reflection, all these years later I suppose the moral of the story is that if you ask a sharp-witted small child a question, they'll assume you don't know the answer so can tell you anything and you'll believe it.

Hard of hearing

As my first daughter, Faye, grew up and learned to talk I found that sometimes she didn't always respond when my wife and I spoke to her. Over a period of time this began to concern me. On one occasion, I crept up behind her and clapped my hands loudly but there was no response from her. For her part while having difficulty with some words her speech progressed fine. I spoke to my wife about this and told her that I thought there was something wrong with her hearing and that we'd probably have to take her to the doctors. I suppose like any worried parent you want to be absolutely certain there's a problem before going to the doctors and I undertook one 'last ditch' effort to check if there really was a problem with Faye's hearing.

Faye was in the bath with the bathroom door open (so my wife could keep an eye on her) and I did my best to creep into the bathroom and since she was facing the other way, she wouldn't have seen me. Then in a gentle whisper I spoke the words 'Daddy's got sweets'. Quick as a flash and with a splashing sound my daughter had turned around, looked at me and said 'want some'. I can't recall how disappointed my daughter was not to have any sweets but I was very pleased my own evidence proved the diagnosis of 'selective hearing' and no visit to the doctors needed to be made.

Christmas chocolates

One Christmas we were at the in-laws enjoying their lavish hospitality, including a good deal of confectionery. Faye was about four or five years old and pretty much eating as much as she could, although I was keeping an eye on her. Somebody opened a box of chocolate liqueurs and I had one or two. Faye 'clocked' them and picked one up to eat. I knew the taste wouldn't be pleasant for her so I told her 'they're nasty chocolates' so as to convey to her in the fewest number of words possible that she wouldn't like them. While she said nothing, she gave me an accusing look as if I had deliberately lied to her and then stuffed a liqueur in her mouth. She soon gave a cough and spat the 'nasty chocolate' out (possibly into the palm of my hand). She said nothing more about this but soon found something else more pleasing to her palate.

Responsibilities of a shareholder

Soon after Faye was born, I opened some savings accounts for her, one of which was a Nationwide account. Every month I paid some money into it and Faye was none the wiser being quite young.

As Faye grew and learned to have a conversation with me it was apparent that she would copy some words and phrases I used. I guess that I either said these words and phrases more often than others, or that she took a liking to them and wanted to use them herself. Sometimes I'd come home from work and ask her what she'd been doing and she'd reply 'I've been to a meeting' at other times she'd tell me that she'd got to go to a meeting. These conversations left me none the wiser as to where or what she been doing but I always thought it was interesting to talk to her. One-day circumstances were such that despite being a toddler she did get an invitation to a meeting, and this is how it happened.

As Faye's savings account was in her name (but with myself as the trustee) any correspondence, at that time, would come to her, in her name, even though she was too young to read or write. She did however, know that the letter 'f' was for Faye. I think in recent years the Nationwide have changed their mailing policy because her younger sister (who was born when Faye was nearly 6) never had the same letters.

One day when a letter arrived for Faye from the Nationwide rather than simply dealing with it myself, on her behalf, I told her: 'Faye, there's a letter for you'. She seemed interested and in reply asked 'what does it say'? I opened the letter and told her 'you've been invited to a meeting' (it was the annual share holders' meeting). Faye paused for a moment before asking 'do I have to go'? No, I told her, not if you don't want to, which seemed to address her concern.

Then, I looked at the papers with the letter and explained she had to vote for some people, and what voting was all about. She asked how to decide who to vote for. In reply I explained that she had to look at photos of the people and if she thought they looked nice vote for them, or against them if she thought they looked nasty. She flicked through the voting pages surprisingly quickly and announced to me that 'they all looked nasty'. I explained that was ok and showed her how we would vote against all of them.

I explained there was also a vote for director's remunerations and she had to decide if it was fair that each person got more money for doing two weeks work, than I got in a whole year. She didn't think that was fair, so we also voted against that. So, with the voting complete, the ballot papers were sealed in the envelope and posted without Faye having to go to a meeting.

Parking trouble in Northampton

I never did find out the name of the woman who lived over the road from us at Northampton, but did notice that one day she'd bought a car. Since it was on 'L' plates I correctly, as it turned out, assumed she was learning to drive. One afternoon on a weekend she decided she needed to move her car from where it was parked in one place in the street, to one nearer her house. I'm not quite sure whether it was myself or Isobel who first noticed this but, in any event, it wasn't long before we were both watching her as she got into a spot of bother. Every manoeuvre she made was wrong and she soon had two wheels of the car on the pavement. Things quickly got progressively worse. Eventually she had most of the car on the pavement such that the passenger door was almost hard up against the door of her own terrace house. At this point I saw her hold her head in her hands and I decided to go across the road and offer some assistance. She readily agreed to my helping her and got out of the car to let me in. It took at least 3 manoeuvres to get the car off the pavement and neatly parked outside her house after which I returned the keys to her and returned home.

Viewing a new house to buy

With a job move and a small promotion, it was time to move house from Northampton to Nuneaton and Faye was six years old at this time. I'd found a house that seemed right for us (we ended up buying a different house) and which I'd had an evening viewing of, on my way home from work. It was now time for Isobel and Faye to look at the house. So, one Saturday we took the train to Nuneaton and walked from the train station to the house. We had explained to Faye we were going to move house but either we'd forgotten to explain the purpose of this visit, or she didn't understand, or wasn't listening. We arrived at the house, rang the doorbell, and the seller of the house invited us in.

The ground floor of the house was a kind of open plan layout with the stairs leading directly off a large lounge. The TV was on and as soon as she saw it Faye slipped from our grasp, ran into the lounge and parked herself in front of it, in an armchair, and began to watch whatever was on. The lady didn't mine at all and showed us the kitchen while Faye watched the TV. When we went to go up the stairs Faye was sufficiently curious to want to go up with us and have a look round. Having now seen both upstairs and downstairs and with Isobel not interested in the garage and my having seen it already, we had completed and viewing, said our thanks, and left. As we walking down the street, back to the train station, Faye was clearly perplexed at the short duration of our visit and asked 'why did we go to see that lady'?

A Visit from the Vicar

As a family we'd moved from a small two-bedroom terrace house in Northampton to a three-bedroom detached house (with a loft conversion fourth bedroom) in Nuneaton, where your money went further buying a house. We'd visited our local Church of England church and decided we'd give it a try. I guess we must have given our details to someone at the church because they'd organised the vicar to visit us.

We had also been given a second-hand microwave at about, or at, the same time. The problem was the microwave didn't fit on the only shelf in the kitchen it might fit on, unless I moved the shelf lower by about an inch so. However, the shelf wasn't easily moved so it was a medium sized piece of DIY work to make it happen.

It also happened that most of the time I don't bother to shave and while I've had and used stubble trimmers from time to time, on the day of the vicar's visit, I simply hadn't shaved for a day or a few days. Because I was engaged in undertaking the DIY job, I was also in scruffy clothes rather than ruin decent clothes.

I paused from my work to introduce myself to the vicar and vice versa. Then he pulled a very sincere caring face of concern and asked me 'Are you in work at the moment?' I laughed and told him I certainly was as I had mortgage to pay. I guess appearances can be deceptive and I found his concern touching. We joined the church and stayed as regular attendees for a number of years until Miranda was a toddler and we felt she needed to be in a church with other young children, which at that time that church sadly didn't have.

Faye – screams

One day I was in the hall of our house just getting ready to go to the shops with Faye. Suddenly, Faye, who was eight years old, 'screamed her head off' and ran to the top of the stairs. When I asked her what the matter was, she replied that there was a big spider. When I asked her where it was, she said it was on my coat. Of course, I was by now wearing my coat!

The works car gets vacuumed

In my day job I very occasionally needed to visit another office and even more occasionally I drove a company car rather than take the train. We had a few cars to choose from and my choice was an old Peugeot that ran and cornered very well. Unfortunately, the Peugeot was unloved and untidy and needed a really good clean. Since I had to keep the car overnight and return it the next day, I decided to get it cleaned out at the garage when I re-fuelled it. So, having refuelled it I asked for a token for the vacuum at the garage only to be told it was out of order. It seemed that the only way I'd get it vacuumed would be if I used our domestic vacuum cleaner when I got home.

Once at home I parked the car on my drive, since my own car was in my garage, and using an extension lead plugged the vacuum in and began to vacuum the car. Our vacuum was a nearly brand-new Dyson and no sooner had I started to use it, the weather changed from overcast to spitting with rain. Since water and electricity don't mix with a good outcome, I decided to put the Dyson into the car, where it would stay dry, carefully perched on the passenger seat. Using the 'stick' tool, perhaps correctly titled by my wife as the 'crevice' tool, I duly vacuumed the car clean.

With the job done it only remained to take the Dyson out of the car, put it away and lock the car. It was as I lifted the Dyson off the seat, I first saw it. 'It' was a bald patch on the seat, rectangular in length and a perfect match for the width of the brush of the Dyson. It seemed that while using the 'stick' tool the brush of the Dyson had continued to rotate and had eaten up all the upholstery from the seat cover and exposed the foam underneath it. Did this unexpected efficiency of the Dyson needed to be explained or not I wondered, but in the end given the age of the car, the next day I confessed all to my boss who fortunately didn't seem duly concerned and nothing more was said about it.

Spa, Belgium (18 May 2001)

I got off the train and looked around. Rucksack, yes, wife, yes, kid, yes, suitcase, no. I realised that we didn't have the suitcase and as I thought about making a dash for the train doors, I saw them close, followed by the departure of the train. Bad news I thought but not a disaster, I'll get 'someone' to pull our suitcase off the train at its next stop, get them to put it on a train coming back here, and we'd just have to suffer waiting around. At the station, we were eventually pointed in the direction of someone who could both understand and speak English. I was surprised because I thought everyone 'abroad' spoke some English. I explained that we (actually me) had left our suitcase on the train. His reply which while correct, didn't convey the empathy he had perhaps intended: 'what a pity', he said. I paused, making an adjustment to match his words to his probable attempt at sympathy and suggested he ring the next station to remove our case. 'That train goes to Germany' he replied and my heart sank. He also explained that the Germans would remove the case and impound it, so it couldn't send it back to Belgium. I thanked him for his help and was reassured by having taken out travel insurance and mindful we had a connecting train to catch to get to Spa. On the final and connecting train my wife sobbed and apologised for having left the case on the train. I reassured her that it was not her fault and that it had been my responsibility to take the case off the train, which it was.

Arriving at Spa I decided the best thing would be to report our loss to the police and get some kind of police report. I was surprised at the police station to find that no-one spoke or understood much English. The police (a small crowd of them) had established I wanted to report the loss of something. More than once they said passports and I shook my head as they were in my camera rucksack. Eventually the Inspector arrived and he understood and spoke more English than his men did. He agreed to write me a report and advised he would be back in a minute. His colleagues laughed at this and kept repeating 'in a minute'. I guess that maybe he didn't usually rush to do things. He was however, fairly quick and handed me the report for which I thanked him. I was a little surprised to see that it had been typed (on a manual typewriter by the look of it) in French.

Our next task was to shop for replacement stuff. A quick scout round Spa established that it was a small town with no department stores but some (in fact two) boutique type clothes shops. The shop staff were very welcoming and no doubt pleased by such a lot of business on what might otherwise have been a quiet afternoon. Certainly, the clothes including my tee shirts and boxer shorts were really good quality and like all good sales staff selling clothing, were spot on finding the right sizes for all three of us (yes, even Faye had new clothes). We never did get our case back again and were very glad we'd taken out travel insurance.

The Mamod stationary steam engine

As a kid I had a Mamod stationary steam engine that my Dad bought me for Christmas one year. He probably bought this from a toy shop that had lots of Mamod and Mecanno called 'Oliver Carley's'. It hadn't been unwrapped and out of the box very long before, when for some reason, the decision was taken to screw it into a small pastry board. The engine would drive accessory tools and I'd also received a small accessory, a wheel driven (via a cam) hammer, to go with it, that was also screwed to the board. Putting an elastic band on the flywheel of the steam engine to the flywheel of the hammer, enabled the steam engine to drive the hammer by operating via the cam which was on a common shaft with the flywheel. The heat to turn the boiler water into steam on the steam engine, came from a small burner. The burner was filled with methylated spirits, purple in colour, rather than coal to burn, to provide the heat.

During the course of my childhood every now and then I'd want to get the steam engine going, only to find I had run out of meth's. My parents would give me some money and I'd take the empty bottle to the chemists on a local 'parade of shops' to get it refilled for about thirty-five pence. The routine was always similar in that I'd ask the assistant for some meth's and they'd then fetch the chemist from the back of the shop. He was an old balding white-haired man with small glasses. He'd move his glasses slightly down his nose so he could peer over the top of them and then he'd ask me what I wanted the meth's for. I'd explain I wanted them for my steam engine and he'd tell me I wasn't old enough to buy meth's but he'd let me this time. I never did get old enough for this procedure to cease, all the years I lived in Peterborough. As the years passed and my life changed, the Mamod steam engine pretty much got forgotten. Then one day when I was browsing the shops in Birmingham, where I now worked, I saw a whole selection of Mamod engines. That evening I decided to get my old steam engine working to show Faye who at that time was about five or six years old. The problem was that no matter how hard I looked, and no matter where I searched, I couldn't find it. Eventually a vague recollection that I'd given it away, when we lived at Courteenhall, Northamptonshire, surfaced in my memories and I was resigned to it having gone forever. A solution was at hand in the form of 'e-bay' and soon Faye and I were bidding on Mamod steam engines until we eventually 'won' an auction and after paying for it, it duly arrived in the post.

Now being of an age when buying Meth's wasn't a problem and having bought some, I gave the engine a quick once over to make sure the boiler pressure relief valve worked and applied some grease or Vaseline to the piston and cylinder. This little stationary steam engine was then duly placed on the back-door kitchen mat, the kitchen back door opened, the burner filled, lit and put in position, and 'steaming up' began. It had been twenty or more years since I'd last done this and some happy memories came flooding back.

Then all of sudden I realised something was wrong. There was a smell of burning that didn't seem correct. I removed the burner from under the boiler and there it was, a large melted area of kitchen mat! I quickly re-positioned the engine outside on a paving slab and 'steaming up' recommenced. I looked at the kitchen mat and it was obvious the heat from the burner had melted it and had I not intervened; the mat might have caught fire. I recalled at this point that my engine had only ever been run screwed to a wooden pastry board and perhaps that was why the base of the engine had a hole pattern like Mecanno because it was not designed to be free standing, but screwed to something. Faye was only vaguely interested in the engine and asked "will it go round and round"? "No" I replied "It just stays where it is". In fact, I think she asked the same question at least once more, perhaps because she thought it ought to propel itself around our garden and was perhaps a little bit disappointed that it didn't. Later that week, I purchased a new kitchen door mat.

A socket set

I was busy doing something in the garage one day and Faye who was probably about ten years old came to see what I was up to, which was somewhat uncharacteristic of her as she rarely came down the garden path to the garage. Part of my tool kit is a fairly old 3/8" drive Kamasa socket set which isn't that special, but still looks reasonably shiny in its green plastic 'blow moulded' case. Faye saw the shiny sockets in the case and said 'wow'. Then after pausing a moment she asks "who, err, who…" Having believed I'd correctly anticipated her question I say: "who gets these after I'm dead"? Faye looks at me and says "well, yeah". You can have them if you want darling, I tell her somewhat bemused. So then, having staked her claim on my cheap Kamasa socket set, she said 'goodbye' and I continued with whatever I was doing in the garage.

The woman on the train

On my daily commute to work on the train, I prefer to sit on my own in an aisle seat, rather than a set of four seats with or without a table. Some days that isn't possible either because the train is fairly full when I get on it and I have to sit next to someone else, or I get the aisle seat on a set of two empty seats and someone wants to sit at the empty seat next to mine. I'm never keen on sitting at a set of four seats, with or without a table as there's less leg room, so that's pretty much the seat of last resort for me.

Sometimes you can tell the train is going to be busy, meaning it has more passengers than usual, because there will be a larger number of people on the platform than usual. One particular morning there were three women, early twenties I guess, who appeared to have been out clubbing or partying all night and found themselves at Nuneaton station on their journey home. They weren't particularly drunk, just a bit on the noisy side.

The train arrived and since the doors stopped about where I expected them to, I was one of the first, if not the first, on. The carriage was fairly full and the only seat I could find was a set of four without a table. I'm guessing the table had been removed because it was broken because the rolling stock used on my normal commute doesn't usually have a set of four seats, two seats facing two seats without a table. I wouldn't have been at my seat for long before the three women filled the empty seats. This didn't bother me and I simply slipped into my normal routine of reading the newspaper.

I can't remember if the woman sitting closely opposite me was trying to talk to me or not, but if she was, I didn't respond. I do remember that she touched my knee. Well, people do accidentally touch each other on the train from time to time, so I ignored it. Then she kept putting her hand on my knee and I ignored that as well. Then she put her hand on my knee and began to slowly move it up the inside of my thigh! I put my paper down and said 'hello'. She laughed and said 'hello' back and then we talked all the way to Birmingham New Street. Her two friends were asleep most of this time, though one did wake up and shout-sing just as we were pulling into the station.

At the end of the day, back at home with my family I thought it best to explain to my wife that an unknown woman had unsolicited placed her hand on my knee and then my inner thigh. My wife thought this was very funny. However, Faye who was probably about eight or even ten years old was furiously angry – 'how dare she do that. Why did you let her? You should have called the police. Don't ever let anyone do this again. Call the police next time you see her' she told me. I did try to explain it was no big deal but she remained cross about this before storming off to another part of our house.

Customer Service

I'd gone shopping and taken Faye with me who was probably aged about nine or ten years old and we were in Halfords, Nuneaton. I can't remember what I was buying but when I got to the checkout it wasn't manned. I waited a while and looked around the store expecting to see a keen shop assistant heading in the direction of both myself and the checkout. Unfortunately, I couldn't see any assistants walking in my direction but did see a couple of them talking to each other. They didn't see me on the other side of the store or if they did, it made no difference to them.

I'm not always the most patient of people and I got fed up of waiting for them. Unfortunately, I recall that I really did need what I'd planned to purchase. So, in a moment of inspiration I leaned over the counter and moved the microphone for the store's public-address system near enough for me to speak into. I found the switch to press when talking and calmly made the following announcement: Customer service assistant to the checkout please', twice. I then returned the microphone to its original position and waited. Quite soon a young and bemused looking Halfords employee arrived at the checkout. She politely took my credit card for the transaction and while she did so Faye kept squeezing my hand. Faye squeezing my hand was her way of sending me a very important 'message' when she didn't want to speak. With my transaction complete I left the store.

As soon as we were outside Faye, squeezed my hand again while trying to drag me up the road. I laughed. She told me to hurry up and I asked her what the rush was. She told me that we needed to get a move on before the police arrived. I laughed again and asked why the police would come and she told it was because I shouldn't have touched the microphone and made the announcement. I laughed even harder but she didn't relax until we were well out of sight of the store. She remembers this to this day, and recalls how the customer behind us also laughed when I made the announcement. Finally, I'm pleased to say that I never needed to make a similar announcement since.

A visit to the Doctors

On the twenty third of December one year which fell on a Thursday, it was my first day off work for the Christmas break. I woke up with a neck ache and head ache. Because I was a bit bunged up, I wondered if it was sinusitis and inhaled some menthol crystals. As the day wore on, I felt worse and took a pink Migraleve pain-killer tablet at about half past nine. Later in the morning I thought I'd better make a doctors' appointment, and did, in case it was sinusitis or an ear infection and I needed antibiotics, as well as not wanting to be really ill over Christmas.

At some point in the afternoon I was sick, several times and felt really ill and in a lot of pain. After a break from being sick I took another pink Migraleve. It was soon time for the doctors' appointment, and my older daughter, Faye, came with me in case I collapsed on the way or something, as well as bringing a carrier bag for me to be sick into, and some loo roll for wiping up! At the doctors, we were directed to the upstairs waiting room. I looked around and there were no toilets. It was a long wait (thirty minutes) as the doctor was running late with her appointments. Feeling worse than ever it was finally my turn to see the doctor. Faye stayed in the waiting room.

The doctor (was a young woman) wanted to check my blood pressure and pulse which were both fine (I'd not expected her to need to check them but then I'm not a doctor). She said I didn't have either an ear infection or sinusitis which was good news. By this time, though I was still really suffering and felt terrible.

Then, I'm not certain if I stood up and announced I was going to be sick, or announced I was going to be sick and stood up, I think it was the latter. I walked towards, and looked into the doctor's sink and the doctor looked and me but said nothing. There was some kind of complicated looking metal apparatus in the sink. I took the doctor's silence as a discouragement from being sick in the sink. I was vaguely aware that at this point she had left the room. I looked at the wastepaper basket not too far from the sink. I bent down and lifted the bag of contents from the wastepaper basket and placed it near the position the bin had originally occupied. Then I commenced to be sick into the bin. Whether or not the doctor was surprised when she returned to her surgery room to find her patient on his hands and knees being sick into her wastepaper bin I'll never know. Some paper towels fluttered down to the left of me, and in between gasping to get my breath back I used one to wipe my mouth. There wasn't a great deal of sick in the bin and it looked fairly watery, though I could see what must have been the remains of the pink Migraleve. Having been sick I immediately felt ever such a lot better.

She gave me a prescription for 'Bucasan' and said I might have had some sort of virus as well as a migraine. My thoughts were that I'd just had a bad migraine after all, because I suddenly felt a lot better (par for the course for a migraine for me is to feel better after being sick). I 'collected' Faye from the waiting room and as we left the doctor's surgery I asked her if she heard me being sick. Her response was that 'everyone in the waiting room could hear you being sick'. And so, feeling a lot better and slightly amused, I was now ready for Christmas.

The Bull Mastiff club of America

One year we had a family holiday to America staying at a convention centre near Hershey, Pennsylvania. We were there for a car show and a classic car meet. Probably because of the way we had to book our flights we arrived before our 'convention' but near the end of one for the Bull Mastiff dog club of America. I don't know much about dogs but rightly guessed the Bull Mastiff is a large breed of dog.

A lot of the owners seemed to either keep the dogs in their room some, or all of the time, and I recall walking past one room where the door was open and peering in. The occupants seemed to have a very large cage they kept a very large dog in. Certainly, there was a very pungent odour of dog in the corridors of the convention centre. Eventually the dog event finished and our car meet started. However, on that weekend the car meet wasn't the only event as a wedding reception was also being held there. One late afternoon we were first intrigued, and then amused, to see a large crowd of people inside and outside one particular room. It seemed the new occupants of the room were less than pleased with the room they had been allocated and a small group of friends, and possibly the venue staff, were dealing with the issue. We only heard a couple of comments which were delivered in a broad American accent. The first was 'gee it really stinks in there' and the other was 'did they have a dawg in the room'? We laughed and laughed, knowing that there certainly had been a dog in the room, lots of rooms in fact!

The kitchen ceiling

As I walked into the Kitchen at our home in Nuneaton, England, I was startled to see a lot of water running down the wall above the back door and water dripping through a very wet and sagging ceiling. I ran upstairs to the bathroom where Miranda (probably about five or six years old) was having a bath. The bathroom floor was absolutely sopping wet. Miranda seemed her usual cheerful self. There was no obvious reason for the flood and rather than the bath being full to overflowing, it was in fact at a reasonable enough level.

I asked Miranda what had happened to cause so much water to be on the bathroom floor. She explained that she climbed up onto the edge of the bath and jumped in which had caused the flood. Somewhat surprised by this explanation I enlisted Isobel's help to do whatever possible to dry the floor. Returning downstairs, a gentle poke with a broom handle brought down a very large area of what was once the kitchen ceiling. Eventually the ceiling was repaired with a large piece of plasterboard and Miranda restricted her jumping into water to the swimming pool.

The caravan keys

Since Faye had been quite small, we'd taken our annual family holiday on the Isle of Wight staying at a caravan park within walking distance of the beach. With Miranda's arrival, nothing changed and one year she was old enough to run around short distances and was still learning to speak – she was probably just under two years of age. Miranda had a very determined character and unlike her older sister, was less keen on talking and telling you what she was thinking.

While the caravan park was a safe environment there was a small brook nearby and also a busy main road (or what passes for one on the Island). I decided, since we didn't have a playpen with us, that we'd always keep the caravan door shut and locked to keep Miranda in. However, we'd also always leave the keys in the lock so that in any kind of emergency, such as a fire, we could quickly get out. No sooner was the door locked and the keys in the lock, Miranda took an immediate interest in them. She stood by the door and reached up to the keys and rattled them. I laughed at her and told her 'you won't be able to unlock it'. Miranda ignored me.

After this, every day when we were in the caravan, Miranda would spend a lot of time rattling the keys, ignoring any remarks I made and even preferring this activity to watching television. I think it was about the Thursday when I heard the door of the caravan open. I quickly ran to the door and went outside to see Miranda just going around the corner of the caravan laughing. It had taken her nearly all week but her determination had finally paid off. A few days later and back at home I looked in the 'baby book', a kind of instruction manual for new parents which warned that when children were nearly three years old they would be able to unlock doors with keys – so she was well advanced on that score.

The cot

As a toddler, Miranda was never very keen on going to sleep once she'd been put in her cot and it wasn't look before she used to try and get out. Her technique was to try and lift herself up the side of the cot. She used to spend a lot of time doing this and most nights I used to laugh at her and say 'you won't be able to get out' to which her response was to ignore me and keep trying. One evening I was in the lounge and thought I could her noises upstairs from Miranda's bedroom. I went upstairs and sure enough there she was looking very pleased with herself and having a little run around her bedroom. I can't remember how old she was but certainly she wasn't yet able to talk, though did understand much of what was said to her.

I picked her up and put her back in the cot and then said "can you show me how you got out?" She immediately started to try and lift herself up the side of the cot and quickly managed to balance her stomach on the cot bar and then did a back-flip onto a full-size bed which was beside her cot. I was amazed at this and decided it would be best if I left the cot side down so she could get in and out without the risk of having a back-flip go wrong.

Later, every evening, once she'd gone to sleep, I'd put the cot side up so she didn't fall out of the cot in the night. One evening she must have woken up after I'd put the cot side back up, exited with a back flip and then decided she wanted to get back in the cot. The first I knew about this was when I heard a loud crash. I went to Miranda's room and while she was in the cot it didn't look right. A closer investigation revealed the metal spring base of the cot was broken at one end from what I could only assume was Miranda jumping back in over the top. So, the cot was now wrecked and while she was still only very small it was time for her to sleep in her 'big bed'.

That's odd

Early one evening in the summer I was in the lounge when unexpectedly the lights went out. 'That's odd' I announced. I think we noticed some more lights went out which also seemed odd. Then Faye, aged about ten or eleven, and quicker on the up-take than my wife or I, shouted out 'Miranda'. I ran out of the lounge and just around the corner there was Miranda. She had discovered the wooden wall mounted box that housed the electric meter and consumer unit and opened it. She'd also opened the plastic over on the consumer unit. Lastly, she'd discovered the trip switches for each electric circuit and was quietly flicking down each switch. After that I had to fit a special 'Miranda proof' lock to the box and several other doors that contained things such as the central heating controls I didn't want switched.

In recalling this story I'm not certain if it occurred before or after our holiday in a caravan on the Isle of Wight when Miranda discovered the hot water boiler controls for the caravan and managed to switch it off. The site warden patiently, but with some difficultly, managed to re-set it and get it going again but it appeared not to be an easy task for him and he looked unhappy, unlike Miranda.

Purple Bunny

When Faye was at primary school, she would be collected at the end of the day by Isobel who would necessarily take Miranda along with her in her pushchair. I guess that some days Miranda would take a soft toy with her, of which she had a large number.

On those rare days when I wasn't working, I'd go with Isobel and Miranda to collect Faye. Once, just as we'd crossed a main road thanks to the Lollipop lady, she asked us if this was ours and held up a soft toy. I didn't recognise it but Isobel did and it was indeed one of Miranda's soft toys. It was fairly muddy and had to go in the washing machine when we got home.

We guessed that on some previous trip to collect Faye from school Miranda had thrown the soft toy out of the pram where it landed on the edge of someone's garden. The soft toy was a purple rabbit which we called purple bunny. From that day forward, I always told Miranda that once purple bunny had once lived in a garden just like a real rabbit.

The Toaster

By the time Faye was a teenager so was our toaster, having been a wedding present. Unfortunately, while it still toasted ok it had long ceased to hold toast down so had to be given manual assistance in the form of a wooden spatula. The routine was to insert the bread into the toasting slot, press the lever down, and then wedge the operating lever down with the wooden spatula. In fact, this routine was probably the only one Faye had ever known for using the toaster, and there were few problems in this routine.

Then one Sunday afternoon I was upstairs having a snooze and my wife and younger daughter were at the park. I was awoken by several things happening all at once: Faye shouting for help, at least two, if not three, smoke detectors in the house sounding an alarm, and the smell of toast burning. I quickly ran downstairs while Faye ran into the lounge, closing the door behind her.

I opened the kitchen door and entering this smoke-filled room shut the door behind me. I immediately grabbed the toaster and both switched and unplugged it from the socket. Very quickly the kitchen re-filled with smoke, my having released some of it when I entered the kitchen, and I could not see my finger in front of my nose. Our kitchen is not large but it took me a while to feel my way to the back door, then find the handle and then open the door. Once I had done this, the smoke cleared a bit and I picked up the toaster again, having put it down while I searched for the door, and threw it outside onto the patio. I could see that even the plastic part of the toaster was now on fire so it was clearly time to 'retire' the spatula and buy a new toaster.

Once the drama was over (which was shorter than the length of time the house smelt of burned toast) I found Faye, who was crying. I asked her what the matter was and she was concerned I would be angry with her and was somewhat surprised when I casually announced there was nothing to worry about and I'd simply buy a new toaster.

Pepper pot at the Isle of Wight

I've wanted to visit this monument: http://en.wikipedia.org
/wiki/St.Catherine's Oratory, on the Isle of Wight, England, known as the
'Pepper pot' for some years on our annual holiday. Finally, not only were we
all back at the Isle of Wight for a holiday but had time to visit the 'Pepper pot'.
So, setting out with a map, which I subsequently left in the car by mistake,
passed through a gate on a public footpath into a foggy field. The family were
with me as we climbed up a foggy hillside. It wasn't long before looming up
out of the fog was a really big cow which I soon realised was in fact a bull! I
think this is the first time I've been in the same field as a bull and I admit now,
I was scared (but not at the time to the family) but not scared enough to go
back since the bull seemed disinterested in us. Further into the field and
further up the hillside were cows, some with calves. The fog was just as thick
as we worked steadily upwards, around the grassy edge of some kind of gorge
till we eventually found the monument, looming large out of the fog, making
for interesting if not great photos and a story to tell about it afterwards.

Lost

We were at Black Gang Chine, which is an adventure park, on the Isle of Wight, England, and were at Miranda's (aged 13 years old) favourite part which was Cowboy Town. After Miranda had charged around for a long time, wearing her cowboy outfit, and used up several packets of caps in her toy cowboy six shooter, she joined us for a break and to explore the other parts of cowboy town including the shooting gallery.

At one point she was looking around as if she'd lost something. So, I asked her 'have you lost something Miranda?' She replied that she'd just seen this really handsome Dad and was trying to find him again. I asked 'is it me?' to which she replied no, of course not, or some equally amusing but candid reply.

Miranda's big sister, Faye, told me that she thought all this was very funny because just as Miranda was telling me this the handsome Dad in question walked by!

Nissan Micra R at the test track

As a freelance motoring writer, I was invited annually, to attend a day at the test track where it was possible to drive pretty much any car on track or off road, and I did. One year there was a very special car called the Nissan Micra R which was a substantially modified car with the engine and powertrain all being a direct transplant from a works Nissan racing touring car.

It seemed clear to me that this would be a popular car and that I'd better drive it early on in the day before there was a long wait to get to drive it. As things turned out I was the first person to drive it which posed its own problems for me as I hadn't had chance to re-learn the layout at the test track so would have to drive a little more carefully and slowly than I'd have liked and of course while getting used to the car as well. The car had a sequential gear shift with dog engagement which meant gear changes without the clutch were possible. From memory it was push the lever to change up and pull to change down, or was it the other way around? In any event as I drove the car, I remembered we were coming up to a section where there was a tight right-hand corner followed by a steep uphill section. So I decided I'd give the car full throttle as soon as I was clear of the corner exit to see just how quick the car would accelerate.

As I arrived at the corner, I put my plan into action and being at a reasonable speed in 2nd car, accelerated out of the corner by flooring the throttle. Several things then happened at once. The engine rpm screamed and the passenger/pro driver supervisor banged the gear lever forwards at least twice. I realised that rather than changing up on a near full throttle in 2nd gear I had in fact changed down to first and the pro-driver changed up rapidly back to 2nd and then 3rd if not 4th. I couldn't tell what revs the engine had pulled as it had a digital LCD bar display a bit like a 1970s Austin 1300 saloon rather than a dial display. While still driving the car, so clearly the engine had survived, I made a tacit enquiry if the engine was ok. My passenger replied calmly but with an edge of irritation in his voice, that 'it was ok'. I drove steadily after that and thanked the passenger as I returned the car to Nissan and made a sharp exit.

A loose electrical socket at work

At my place of employment I'd worked for one manager for many years and over those years got used to him and some of his ways, for want of a better phrase. One thing he was always really keen on was never fiddling with computers or electrical equipment himself, or letting anyone else, including me, do so either, even though I built my own home computers from components. I guess over the years he become increasingly frustrated with the level of service he'd received from the IT department of our employer, specifically the time it took before it was delivered. I wasn't really aware of this until one day he asked me to have a look at a computer that had stopped working. I was surprised to be asked, given his previous stance on this type of issue, but agreed to do so.

As I crawled under the desk, I found a lead wasn't plugged in properly and rectified it. However, without a further second's thought I leant up and did my first ever impression of someone receiving an electrical shock (I'd had a couple of real ones over the years so knew what to do). As I looked across at my manager, I saw his jaw drop and a look of horror pass across his face. I couldn't help myself from ceasing doing the impression to laugh my head off. I'm not really sure if he saw the funny side of the joke or was so relieved, he hadn't actually caused me to get an electrical shock he couldn't tell me off for it. Either way, it was the funniest thing I'd experienced in a long time and one that sticks in my memory.

The Cockroach

I was in my garage one evening, converting a fluorescent tube fitting to work with an LED tube, when Faye (18 years old) burst in, sobbing. I was startled and thought something serious had happened, a death in the family or something like that. However, Faye explained there was a cockroach in her bedroom. This didn't seem very likely to me and I guessed it was some kind of large beetle that had decided to spend the winter somewhere relatively warm. Once in the house Faye explained the 'roach was behind her bedroom door and I was surprised that it was still there and went to get a bright torch to shine on it. I also asked Faye to get the vacuum cleaner as I planned on sucking it up with the vacuum cleaner. So, torch at the ready and crevice tool applied to the cleaner's hose, I was ready to meet the 'roach.

Yep, it was a real big one, bigger than the biggest ones I'd seen on Ascension Island, let alone in the Philippines, but oddly, was totally black. It didn't move and the crevice tool sucked up and held it, since it was too large to go up the pipe at the angle, I'd caught it at. It didn't move as I took a closer look at it and as I suspected it was a Chinese cockroach, well it was made in China, injection moulded most likely. Faye was both relieved, cross and amused at the same time at her younger sister, Miranda (age 13), for planting it in her room. Miranda was simply amused.

A plug-in air freshener

In one corner of our kitchen we have a wall mounted double electric plug socket. The sockets weren't used for much until we recently acquired a plug-in air freshener. And, not long after that, a spider took up residence behind the plug-in air freshener and seemed happy there. To the unknowing and untrained eye, he might as well not have been there at all.

Now, I'm not that troubled by spiders and my wife will even catch one in her hand and then deposit it in the garden, unharmed by it running around in her partially closed hand looking to escape. However, my two daughters, are not keen on spiders. So, after a few days of seemingly being the only person to notice the spider I asked my daughters if they could unplug the air freshener for me and take a look at it (the air freshener). My older daughter duly unplugged it and then screamed loudly as she dropped it on the floor while the younger daughter who was also peering closely at it screamed as well. Both the air freshener and the spider survived being dropped onto our tiled kitchen floor.

Dad Knew Best

As a kid growing up, I enjoyed many great annual family holidays on the Isle of Wight. For each holiday I had extra pocket money to spend and some of it always got spent on a cheap penknife. The knives varied in appearance but were pretty much the same basic knife that wasn't very sharp and which the shiny sides fell off within months if not weeks. One year Dad took me to a shop that sold Victorinox pocket knives – the original Swiss Army knives. He explained they were a very good knife and that I ought to buy one in preference to buying my annual cheap 'fare'. I wasn't keen on the idea, being old enough to realise the purchase would cost virtually all my holiday money and leave me with no money left for anything else. Then he applied some parenting pressure that as a kid I was unable to withstand and I ended up buying an expensive two-blade Alox Victorinox penknife that I didn't really want to pay for.

Back home after the holiday I quickly grew to like my Victorinox Swiss Army knife and told my school chums what a great knife it was and probably showed them it at school as well. However, somewhere along the years of my using it, I managed to damage it, bending over one end slightly and consequently the blades no longer folded back in the way they were supposed to without fiddling about with them. I grew into adulthood and car ownership and the knife found its way into the selection of tools I carried in my car and was forgotten about for many years, most likely more than a decade if not two decades.

Then one day while reducing the number of tools in my car tool kit I found the knife of my boyhood, 'rescuing' it and putting it in a desk drawer in my home where it was forgotten once more for many years.

In 2017 I bought my younger daughter a Victorinox Swiss multi tool which she was pleased with, as one of her Christmas presents. Not long after that I decided to treat myself to several Victorinox knifes, including a Swiss Champ. I also watched a YouTube video all about Victorinox and near the end of the clip I learned that their products are guaranteed for life and can be overhauled or repaired. Some subsequent research on my part led me to learn that if a knife has been damaged from sort of mistreatment it can still be repaired but for a small fee.

Days later, care of the UK importer, my little penknife was heading back to Switzerland to return to the hands of its creators! Weeks later I duly paid a small repair fee and after a while, the knife was back with me. I'd already learned its aluminium body couldn't be re-anodised but, in a way, I was glad that was so, because its appearance and character would have changed. So, now back in my sometimes-clumsy hands it still looked like my knife of my boyhood that it was. The blades were now sharp and open and closed as if they were brand new. The bent end was much less bent and one rivet looked new. But best of all I now have the happy memory that my Dad knew best. The Victorinox penknife was money well spent, and it makes me smile whenever I pick up the knife whether I'm going to use it or not.

Printed in Great Britain
by Amazon

59724466R00071